Reconstructing Memory:

Black Literary Criticism

D1605613

Reconstructing Memory:

Black Literary Criticism

Fred Lee Hord, Ph.D.

THIRD WORLD PRESS • Chicago

Reconstructing Memory:
Black Literary Criticism

by Fred Lee Hord, Ph.D.

THIRD WORLD PRESS
CHICAGO, ILLINOIS

First Edition 1991
First Printing 1991
ISBN: 0-88378-144-1
LC#: 89-050683

Cover illustration by Joey Henderson
Cover design by Cassandra Malone

Manufactured in the United States of America
Third World Press
7524 S. Cottage Grove Ave.
Chicago, Il 60619

To my parents, Rev. Noel E. Hord and Jessie Tyler Hord, and to my children, Teresa Hord Owens, F. Mark Hord, and Laurel E. Hord.

Table of Content

How to Stop the Violence and Learn to Love Your African Self

In the world of RAP music there is a philanthropic, self-help movement called the "stop the violence" movement. Black artists who comprise this movement do not advocate, say, an end to police brutality in
America or a suspension of states of emergency in South Africa.
(Though, surely, their politics would find such advocacy ideologically
correct.) Rather, the "stop the violence" movement announces its theme
as "self-destruction." "I never ran from the Klan/So why should I have to
run from a black man?" they ask. The movement's premise is that black
intraracial and internecine murder of the African in one's self or in the
personhood of one's urbanstreet brothers forecasts racial doom.

In his present volume, Professor Fred Hord lays out a pedagogy of
African-American self-defense against black self-destruction. His book
is about the global dilemma created by Western imperialistic colonialism.

Colonialism first takes control of the Other's land and material resources. Next, it establishes a mystifying ownership over the Other's boy and
mind. What follows is black self-destruction. Such self-destruction takes
the form of subconscious, unconscious, or even blindly wanton endorsement by the Other of the colonizer's symbolic codes — political, social,
economic, cultural, and phenotypic. Frantz Fanon says the black skin
under colonial rule desires the white mask. Hord says that his students at
Howard University hated the African phenotype, preferring fair-skin
soulmates for commerce and culture. (We flash to Langston Hughes's
"The Negro Artist and the Racial Mountain.")

Amilcar Cabral says the cessation of self-destruction is motivated
through one route only — a return to the source — a journey back to
renewing myths of our pre-colonial origins.

Hord argues that an interventionist pedagogy — a new educational RAP, as it were, for New Times — is the only way to stop the violence of black self-destruction. Those who can stop the violence are black educators — teachers who have travelled in what Fanon calls the zone of occult instability where the people dwell.

These educators, in Hord's account, take up the sacred texts of rebellious slaves, resistant poets, cultural Jeremiahs, RAP griots and put them to revolutionary use. Only skilled teachers can extrapolate from placid words and seemingly simple lyrics messages of enduring African significance.

Hord reads Frederick Douglas, Paul Laurence Dunbar, Sonia Sanchez, Haki Madhubuti, and others with the superb wisdom of his own "stop the violence" pedagogy.

He shows us that the beginning of efficacious self-love (as opposed to self-destruction) lies in the powers of memory and desire.

By reconstructing — figuring forth in fine analytical detail — the sweet honey in the rock of our African heritage, Hord provides an empowering sense of an alternative African knowledge for these times. He is a keen writer and an honest rapper. He convincingly demonstrates that a reconstructed memory is the only means through which to stop the violence.

Hord's pedagogical model could not have arrived at a more auspicious moment. In an era of transnational, multi-media colonization of the Other's mind, we desperately require voices such as Hord's. His book comes to us now as a timely and necessary gift in a dangerous hour of forgetting. May the gift be graciously accepted and widely read.

Houston A. Baker, Jr.

Introduction

Although the writer has taught African-American literature and history to black students for twenty years, and has observed the evolution and dissolution of black student consciousness — that sense of rootedness in and clarity about the past which contributes to the cultural re-creation of the myths of African-American identity and ethos — during that period, his three years of instruction at Howard University have crystallized critical issues regarding that consciousness. For the experience of teaching black students exclusively near the end of the '80s provided focus and thus additional insight into the vital intersecting dimensions of racial pride and values. Each semester, students raised questions about their dispositions regarding racial esteem and their praxis of social values. Each semester, in turn, the author raised questions about how they relate to the African-American past, the African phenotype, and the American ethos. The preponderant response was unawareness of the African-American past, disassociation from the African phenotype, and an association with the American ethos. Although the writer's involvement in the African-American struggle as teacher/activist has been useful in assisting black students in deciphering this American side of their cultural duality, what remains particularly bothersome is the historical obfuscation surrounding issues of racial pride and values. In response to students' questions about their role in the "movement," it has been necessary not only to explore the external and internal forces that assaulted black student consciousness during and since the period projected on the recent PBS series "Eyes on the Prize" — especially the internal historical rootlessness reflected in the superficial embracing of Africa and the substantial external pandering to the reformist element of the black middle class — but also to dialogue with black students about connecting that history and its grounding with their own lives. Such reconstruction of memory seems indispensable for their clear assessment of their own predilections regarding racial pride and values.

As the author suggested earlier, the vast majority of more than five hundred students he has taught at Howard University seem confused —

though concerned — about who they are and the propriety of an extreme individualistic/materialistic value system. What is more, they do not appear to understand the implications of identity ambivalence, much less the limited practicability and unlimited danger of their projected attempts to operationalize that value system. For instance, most students become thoughtful when they follow up the writer's recommendation to compare the way they are wearing their hair with Howard students in the 1955 and 1970 yearbooks. Yet, they are not sure what it means that the close-cropped look of the males on campus and the relaxed coiffure of the females resemble the styles of the pre-student movement days. Further, they do not necessarily attach overwhelming identity significance to the afros in the 1970 yearbook. Some insist that current hair styles are merely a matter of vogue; most, however, answer with long silences or concessions that perhaps they are not as secure in their identities as they thought.

Conversely, most students clearly agree that African-Americans have by no means won the color-complex struggle; some openly admit their preferences for light-skinned companions of the opposite gender. A few students even relate stories about parents who unabashedly communicate their partiality toward light skin color. Yet, in spite of their own penchants, most students are aware that the African phenotype ranks at the bottom of the cultural hierarchy in this society. As a prime example, they talk about how the vast majority of *Ebony* models, even if they have deep brown skin, exhibit European features or their approximates.

Not only has the author witnessed a general disassociation from the African phenotype among African-American students at Howard University, but he has also discerned a mixture of nescience of and association with the dominant value system of this society. First, there seems to be little clarity about the capitalistic system, much less their class locus in it or why the underclass is generally not on campus with them. Most students either do not understand what critics mean when they accuse the black middle class in the United States of complicity in the underdevelopment of people of color in the Third World when it uncritically accepts its privileges, or they deny such a connection. Too often, students also communicate the feeling that black folks on the other side of Georgia Avenue could share the harvest of being a Howard student if they became more ambitious.

In addition, strong feelings about returning to the community with their knowledge/skills appear to flourish among few students. Although some grant the unwholesomeness of such a lack of commitment, most are un-apologetic about what they want, and seem quite sure that they will be able to realize their materialistic objectives.

Further, students report that the major dream on campus is the American dream, and that if black communal struggle is in conflict with the pursuit of that dream, there will be no struggle. Each semester, they have informed the writer that a random sampling of Howard students would disclose that from seventy to ninety percent would generally opt for class interests over racial ones. In fact, when I ask them to estimate the number of students who would actually commit what Amilcar Cabral termed class suicide, the percentage plummets to less than five — some-times less than one. Finally, when students have discussed the traditional African value system of communalism reflected in the notion "we are, therefore I am," their responses — in addition to lack of awareness — seem to essentially be either that such a world view today would be hope-lessly naive or that there is nothing fundamentally wrong with the American ethos of individualism/materialism unless perhaps one be-comes obsessed with self or things.

The author's aforementioned observations as instructor — as well as corroborating evidence in voluntary work with student government leaders and in published general analyses of black student consciousness by others like Muhammad Ahmed, S.E. Anderson, K. Sue Jewell, Joseph McCormick, Ronald Walters, and Luke Tripp [1] — have intensified the desire to discover pedagogical methods to access black history. Cog-nizant that all education is political, the increasingly insistent question has become not how one can assure that teaching will insure strong black student consciousness — or even have a predictable impact upon that consciousness — but rather how can it best relate to that consciousness by relating to their concerns. The writer's opinion is that literature can be useful in helping black students to clarify their relationship to the past and thus in making them informed mediators of present issues of racial pride and values.

The vast majority of black students have been removed from their his-tory and have precious little context in which to put the vagaries of their own lives. Their first response to the author's courses has been surprise. Last academic year, the PBS series "The Africans" and "Eyes on the Prize" also elicited awe. The major responsibility for black student ahis-toricity must be attributed to the institutions of this society; however, that does not exonerate those in the institutions who are not resisting the reproduction of cultural repression as well as the reproduction of caste and class hierarchies. Thus, the primary purpose of this book is to help instructors of African-American literature assist black students in understanding their history — especially the myths of black identity and black ethos — and so to aid them in reconstructing memory in such a way to make a valid cultural critique of the past. The impact intended is to thus enable black students to better mediate their cultural duality in the areas of racial pride and values. Instructors should never impose their choices regarding these two issues, but they must assist students in raising alternatives to those choices built into American institutions.

Before briefly describing the pedagogical model of African-American literary criticism which is the fulcrum of this volume, it is necessary to define significant terms, identify the underlying assumptions, and briefly examine the reasons for and the limitations of the study, as well as the rationale for works chosen for analysis in this study.

Nine key terms in this work are culture, myth, generative themes, black identity, black ethos, mystification, dehumanization, cultural duality, and cultural critique. For the heuristic purposes of this analysis, those terms will carry the following definitions:

1) Culture. As African-American literary critic Houston A. Baker, Jr. observed, culture is "a whole way of life grounded in the past."[2]

2) Myth. Slightly modifying literary critic Jane Campbell's definition of myth in her recent work, *Mythical Black Fiction*, the author uses myth "to mean a dramatic embodiment of cultural values, of ideal states of being found in Afro-American history and experience"[3] as reflected or implied in the African-American autobiography, novel, and narrative poetry. More specifically in this study, that embodiment is a literary or critical negotiation of cultural duality and so is a generative theme which proceeds from the demystification and humanization of the colonized. As such, the writer notes with black poet Jay Wright that "myth and history walk hand in hand...(but) that we do not mean anything static"[4] by myth. Thus, as recent Nobel prize winner in literature, Wole Soyinka, puts it, myth emanates from "the cumulative history and empirical observations of the community."[5]

3) Generative themes. According to Brazilian educator Paulo Freire, "the concrete representation of...a complex of ideas, concepts, hopes, doubts, values, and challenges in dialectical interaction with their

opposites, striving toward plenitude...constitute the themes of that epoch."[6] In this study, since "generative themes can be located in concentric circles, moving from the general to the particular,"[7] the fundamental general theme is colonization and its opposite, with its particular themes of mystification and dehumanization and their opposites, and their derivative themes of colonial identity and ethos and their opposites, the myths of black identity and black ethos.

4) Black identity. The myth of rootedness in one's racial past, identification with one's present racial community, and positive association with the African phenotype. The rootedness and identification relate to and overlap with the following term.

5) Black ethos. The myth of commitment to the African communal world view and its extension, the values of African-American communal struggle.

6) Mystification. The institutional efforts of the American colonizers to universalize their particularity by reproducing European-American historical memory and hierarchies of culture, according marginalized status to African-Americans who adopt such memory and accept such hierarchies.

7) Dehumanization. Black identification with the colonizers' historical memory and hierarchies of culture. Such African-Americans who have been granted marginalized status experience what black Caribbean sociologist Orlando Patterson labels"social death," for they cease to belong in their "own right to any legitimate social order."[8] They are no longer subject, but object; he/she has succumbed to the dominant meanings of the colonizer. He/she is (an) other.

8) Cultural duality. The archetypal dialectic between black identity/ethos and colonial mystification/dehumanization.

9) Cultural critique. An analysis of the dialectic of black cultural duality, and its implications for the ordering of African-American political objectives. Other significant terms such as intensive universality, metamorphical event, metamorphical intent, saturation, dialectic of chronological/colonial historicity, and persisting present will be defined in chapter two when the pedagogical model of black literary criticism is fully described.

The primary assumption of this work is that the African-American experience has been and continues to be one of internal colonialism. The author agrees essentially with black cultural historian Harold Cruse "that the only factor which differentiates the Negro's status from that of a pure colonial status is that his position is maintained in the home country in close proximity to the dominant racial group."[9] Subsidiary assumptions are:

    1) Internal colonialism is a form of domestic racist capitalism.

    2) One link between race and class in the African-American experience is the status-ordering system of the colonizer.

    3) Cultural repression through mystification is a critical component of the cultural reproduction of colonial identity and ethos, and pervades the American institution of education.

    4) The cultural repression of American colonial education serves to distort the status perceptions of African-American students by denying and assaulting black identity and ethos, contributing to their cultural duality and potentially to their dehumanization.

    5) Interventive pedagogy in American colonial education is indispensable to African-American student informed mediation of their cultural duality.

    6) Pedagogical intervention should be dialogical as in the manner of Paulo Freire, rather than reflecting the banking concept of education.

    7) African-American literature is a particularly useful resource for pedagogical intervention as it provides access to black history, especially through its embodiment of cultural duality and black identity/ethos.

The above assumptions will be buttressed in chapters one and two.

The pedagogical model of black literary criticism is one which allows the instructor to use the literary texts to explore questions with students which arise from the cultural duality inhering in the cultural repression of African-Americans. More specifically, the instructor may employ this paradigm — which focuses on an archetypal pattern and myths in African-American literature — as a matrix for dialogue with students about their cultural duality and black identity and ethos. That dialogue should be based on the instructor's and students' shared experience of black literary texts as an historical repository, historical texts on the black experience, and the black contexts of their colonized experiences. This model should assist instructors in helping students to relate those three experiences.

The author chose black literature as the vehicle of political socialization because of its relationship to black history, its embodiment of an archetypal pattern and myths, and its potential dramatic impact. Although the writer concedes that black literature is not an exact reproduction of black history, he would agree with Baker that "the Black text is historical evidence because it is a present, palpable component of the past that formed it,....governed by a thinking agent, by the mental life of a culture."[10] He would add with black literary critic Norman Harris that black literature "effervesces with an epistemology that is a true as any utilized by social scientists."[11] Finally, he would suggest that this paradigm allows for the cultural reproduction of the historical dialectic and the examination, if not the cultural re-creation, of the myths of black identitiy and ethos.

The archetypal pattern of cultural duality inheres in this particular situation of internal colonialism. Yes, cultural repression is integral to all colonization, and mystification is often the form that cultural repression assumes. However, in the African-American situation, the configuration of certain historical factors [12] has combined with the fact that the colonized are of African descent and thus have been affected by the disassociation from Africa that was fostered by worldwide European domination of people of color. That is to say that European-American mystification efforts set into motion the archetypal dialectic of cultural duality. Such efforts at mystification and dehumanization were new because these necessary dimensions of subjugation were based on race, as were the African-American responses in creating and reproducing the myths of black identity and black ethos. For the colonized, literature has been one institution that could be employed to re-create, in the words of African art critic Isadore Okpewko, those "progressive forms of communal myth"[13] even when black writers succumbed to the colonizers' mystification and they delineated the dehumanization in their work. And so, those writings can be appropriated as an historical repository to raise questions about how the colonizers' meanings become the dominant ones and why there is a need for African-Americans to re-create the myths of black identity and black ethos.

The potential dramatic impact of African-American literature is also clear. Three black women, who are also educators, writers, and critics, suggest what that impact can be. Howard University professor of education, Nancy Arnez, who is also a literary critic and poet, argues that more emphasis needs to be placed on the fact that "literature through its dramatic impact can inculcate in the reader certain social and anthropological insights which the reader may not glean from reading sociology or anthropology texts."[14] Patently, these insights proceed from the literary text as subtext in the context of readers' experiences, in conjunction with the historical analysis and interaction with the instructor. Coppin State University professor of English, Eugenia Collier, who is a well-known literary critic and short story writer — and to whom we shall return in chapter two — agrees with Arnez about the special dramatic possibilities of literature. Claiming that literature makes the most explicit statement of all the arts, Collier asserts why African-American literature has particular potential for dramatic impact:

> Two hundred years of conscious writing...have yielded a history not to be found in history books, a social commentary not recorded in the sociology texts, an expression of human anguish and endurance not present in volumes of psychology, philosophy, or ethics. [15]

Celebrated poet and literary critic Mari Evans, to whom the writer is in considerable debt for his paradigm of black pedagogical literary criticism (as will be explained in chapter two), not only believes that literature generally provides an intrinsically useful vehicle "for piercing delusion, disseminating information, substituting values, (and) instituting new forms of thought,"[16] but also contends that black literature, by "generating a matrix for national political unity...can play a fundamental role in effecting the transformation from naivete and delusion to political awareness."[17] In fact, Evans proposes that African-American literature "offers...with the help of politically conscious instructors, a laboratory opportunity to open with clinical precision the mind of the Black student and the further privilege to provide for a cleansing, healing, and nurturing process to take place"[18]

Finally, the author submits that the dramatic impact of African-American literature toward political socialization can be best realized in an institutional arrangement. Although the black family, black church, and inner-city public schools represent conceivable structures, he opts for the black college because of its superior intellectual credibility, because that credibility has often been appropriated by the colonizers for heightened mystification, and because there exists some possibility for greater class diversification. Again, the writer suggests that the nature of that pedagogical process of political socialization be dialogical, so that students may be active agents in transforming their inner worlds toward black identity and black ethos, and so may become more catalytic in naming the outside world.

There are four primary limitations of the study. First, this pedagogical paradigm which the author labels metaphorical and metamorphical literary criticism is only a partial and alternative approach to African-American literature. Second, the study only examines the writing of seven authors. Third, the study only reflects literature written from 1845 to 1975. Fourth, the study confines the most recent period it treats (1954-1975) to political artists who were proponents of the Black Aesthetic.

Four points also need to be made about the rationale of the works chosen. First, at least two works represent each of three literary genres; autobiography, poetry, and the novel. Second, at least two works represent each of three historical eras of internal colonialism which the author terms slavery, segregated neocolonialism (1864-1954), and integrated neocolonialism (1954-). Third, writers chosen from the first two periods were four who belong to the traditional canon of African-American literature: Frederick Douglass, Paul Laurence Dunbar, Ralph Ellison, and Maya Angelou. Finally, the author used the three criteria of visibility, rhetorical consistency, and intelligibility to determine the three writers of the last period: John Killens, Sonia Sanchez, and Haki R. Madhubuti (Don L. Lee).

The sequence of the nine chapters and the integral nature of the appendix to the paradigm warrant brief explanations. In the first chapter, the author traces the Third World roots of the internal colonialism model, describes and supports the case for applying that model to examine the African-American experience — including the heuristic advantages — and analyzes the role of institutionalized education in the cultural repression of that colonialism. Chapter two is devoted to the construction of a pedagogical model of black literary criticism rooted both in Third World and African-American colonial theories of literature, as well as in the African-American literary tradition of consciousness raising and collectivity. Chapters three through eight represent applications of the model to the separate texts. Chapter nine is the conclusion; the model is then applied to the intertextualization of all works. The appendix is an integral part of the model, providing accessible historical analyses of the specific periods from the vantage of the colonized, which may serve both as teaching aids for the instructor as well as supplementary reading materials for students. Relevant general historical bibliographies are also included.

Finally, not only does the writer intend positive social impact by attempting to help the instructor assist black students in reconstructing memory, in understanding their own cultural duality, and thus in making an informed cultural critique of their historical experience, but he also trusts that this work will help clarify the African-American experience — and thus the American experience — for others, black and white. By extension, the author hopes that the application of this paradigm to other black literature — especially works written since 1975 — will contribute to the demystification of areas of dehumanization that were not emphasized in the selected literature. Noteworthy among these areas are intraracial problems such as black male sexism, black-on-black crime, drugs, and the symptoms of deteriorating family life. It would be especially gratifying to see the paradigm applied to selected works of the prodigious output by African-American women writers since the cutoff point for this study.

I

Classical Colonialism and African-American Internal Colonialism: Connections

The three most prominent intellectuals of African descent to explore the impact of colonialism on national culture have been Frantz Fanon of Martinique, Albert Memmi of Tunisia, and Amilcar Cabral of Guinea Bissau. Because the major assumption of this study that the historical experience of African-Americans has been one of internal colonialism draws substantially on those progenitors, we need to survey their views on colonialism and culture before we discuss the case for internal colonialism and the related question of American education and cultural repression. In this section of the chapter, the author will describe and analyze the ideas of Cabral, Memmi, and Fanon about the material basis of colonialism, the connections between the colonizers' institutions and racist cultural repression, and the role of national culture in resisting that cultural repression.

The first area of inquiry regards the basis of colonization, and Cabral, Fanon, and Memmi suggest that it is material. Colonization occurs because it is profitable to the colonizing country. Cabral's allusion to the "inescapable contradiction between the colonized society and the colonial power"[1] refers to the economic exploitation of the colonized masses. Fanon reminds us that even when the ruling powers attempt to disguise their oppression by instituting certain reforms, "sooner or later, colonialism sees that it is not within its powers to put into practice a project of economic and social reforms which will satisfy the aspirations of the colonized people."[2] As Memmi indicates, "privilege is at the heart of the colonial relationship — and that privilege is undoubtedly economic."[3] So the three writers agree that the primary motive for colonization is economic.

But, Cabral leads us into our second area of inquiry by insisting that economics is not all. He points up the connections between the material and cultural aspects of domination:

> Whatever may be the material aspect of...domination, it can be maintained
> only by the permanent, organized repression of the cultural life of the people
> concerned. Imperialist domination...requires cultural repression. [4]

Cabral, Fanon, and Memmi understand the inextricability of economics, politics, and culture, and so, the machinations of racist cultural repression. Not only do the colonizers economically exploit the colonized on the basis of race, but they also use the political control which proceeds from their economic power to institutionalize echelons of culture, establishing their racial norms as preeminent.

This racism, Memmi claims, is "one of the best justifications of and symbols for oppression,"[5] which takes "root in the institutions and ideologies all around,...imposing itself on the individual."[6] Cabral maintains that the colonizers create racial theories which "are translated into a permanent state of siege of the indigenous populations on the basis of racist dictatorship (or democracy)."[7] However, he is careful to point out that the colonized who have least connections with the colonizers' institutions are most free from the impact of those theories. So this attempt at what Fanon calls "inferiorization," and Memmi labels "depersonalization" or "dehumanization" is not made on an individual basis; rather, it is structured into the institutions of the colonizer.

Memmi and Fanon are specific about how this institutionalization of racism works. For instance, poor Whites not only benefit economically but also psychologically. Memmi explains:

> To observe the life of the colonizer and the colonized is to discover rapidly that
> the daily humiliation of the colonized, his objective subjugation, are not merely
> economic. Even the poorest colonizer thought himself to be — and actually was
> — superior to the colonized. [8]

The poor whites "are crueler than the rich because they need to maintain and to widen the pathetic distance which separates them from Blacks."[9] Why do poor whites benefit psychologically and gain in status from a system whose fulcrum is economic? In what way does privilege proceed from more than economic imperialism? The one answer to both questions inheres in the racist status ordering-system dimension of the colonizers. As Fanon asserts, "colonialism has never ceased to maintain that the Negro is a savage; and for the colonist, the Negro was neither an Angolan or a Nigerian, for he simply spoke of 'the Negro'."[10] The colonizers institutionalized this idea everywhere and so increased the status of the colonizer everywhere, irrespective of his economic condition. So white skin privilege is both economic and psychological. For as Memmi claims, "the small colonizer defends the colonial system...because he benefits from it to some extent."[11] in economic terms as well as in status. The colonized "is doubly poor; he is the poor man among the poor whites."[12]

Fanon describes the method of colonial inferiorization:

Colonialism....turns to the past of the oppressed people, and distorts, disfigures, and destroys it....When we consider the efforts made to carry out the cultural estrangement so characteristic of the colonial epoch, we realize that nothing has been left to chance and that the total result looked for by colonial domination was indeed to convince the natives that colonialism came to lighten their darkness.... Every effort is...made to bring the colonized person to admit the inferiority of his culture,...to recognize the unreality of his 'nation,' and in the last extreme, the confused and imperfect character of his own biological structure. [13]

Although all institutions work together to mystify and dehumanize the colonized, education can be at once the most subtle yet devastating in its assault on the personality. Memmi explains how colonial education mystifies and dehumanizes the colonized:

The memory which is assigned him is certainly not that of his people. The history which is taught him is not his own....Far from preparing the adolescent to find himself completely, school creates a permanent duality in him. [14]

Sylvia Hill, African-American scholar of Cabral, further clarifies this concept of cultural duality in her discussion of Cabral's notions of the petite bourgeoise as a marginalized class. This element is

a group who, while having a better economic and social status than do the masses, ...can never be equal with the colonizer....Within this class there develops a 'frustration complex' that manifests itself in this need for identity. In search of identity ...the petite bourgeoisie attempts to recapture or search for their lost culture in order to deny the supremacy of the colonizer. [15]

Hill proceeds to explain that "returning to the source is not a 'voluntary step' but is historically determined from the...material reality of their position in relation to the means of production."[16]

Memmi believes that "the most serious blow suffered by the colonized is being removed from history and from the community."[17] He indicates that the tragic consequence of this is that the colonized forgets how to "participate actively in history and no longer even asks to do so."[18] Memmi acknowledges that "memory is not purely a mental phenomenon...That of a people rests upon its institutions."[19] Thus, institutional domination is necessary for the mystification and dehumanization of a people. Conversely, as Cabral notes, cultural resistance of the colonized cannot succeed without preserving their own institutions:

The possibility of a movement group keeping (or losing) its identity in the face of foreign domination depends on the extent of the destruction of its social structure under the stresses of that domination. [20]

It is clear that Cabral, Fanon, and Memmi agree on the link between economics, politics and culture in colonial situations. Cultural repression is part and parcel of colonialism; it is as necessary as arms for waging war. Through institutions, especially education, the colonizer designs to deracinate the past of the colonized, or at least to disfigure the collective memory. The colonizer's meanings must be dominant to mystify the colonized when weakening or supplanting their institutions. Although the basis of colonialism is material, the superstructure of politics and culture is critical to its functioning.

If the politics of institutional domination is the necessary stratagem for cultural repression, then the culture of the colonized must provide some political clues to their successful resistance against the repression. Cabral is most lucid here. He argues generally "that any attempt to clarify the true role of culture in the development of the (pre-independence) liberation movement can make a useful contribution to the broad struggle against imperialist domination."[21] How does one ascertain the "true role of culture" in the politics of liberation, the freeing of the colonized mind from the tyranny of the colonizer's meanings? Again, Cabral points the way:

> It must be noticed that the analysis of the culture gives at once an idea of the strengths and weaknesses of the people, faced with the demands of the struggle, and constitutes a valuable acquisition concerning the stratagems and tactics to follow... on the political plane. [22]

These two statements by Cabral suggest the third area of agreement: the need for a knowledge of the evolving national culture vis-a-vis colonial cultural repression.

Cabral, Fanon, and Memmi each address the issue of national culture and its significance in the struggle toward liberation. Fanon alleges that "every culture is first and foremost national."[23] He then defines national culture:

> A national culture is the whole body of efforts made by a people in the sphere of thought to describe, justify, and praise the action through which that people has created itself and keeps itself in existence. [24]

Cabral relates national culture to the liberation struggle:

> The liberation struggle is, above all, a struggle both for the preservation and survival of the people and for the harmonization and development of these values within a national framework. [25]

Memmi, though also stressing the importance of national culture in the colonial struggle, discerned that the bourgeoisie of the colonized were coming to power in the newly independent countries. He suggests that "most colonies, in gaining independence, have given precedence to form (national) over content (social),"[26] adding that he had predicted "that the domination of one people by another would resolve itself, first of all, into national liberation."[27] The inference is that a cultural critique of the national culture is necessary before nominal independence if there is to be authentic liberation. Although Memmi is warning us of the possibilities of neo-colonialism — that situation where the colonized elite use the trappings of power for their own aggrandizement as well as for the perpetuity of the colonizer — inherent in colonialism and a nationalistic response to it, he does not advise that the national period be omitted in the struggle toward internationalism. As we have observed, Cabral and Fanon concur. Further, Fanon brands as pharisees those who aver that the national period should be skipped, that it is "a phrase that humanity has left behind, [that] it is the day of great concerted actions, and retarded nationalists ought in consequence to set their mistakes aright. "[28] Fanon insists that there is no contradiction between national culture and internationalism:

> Culture is the expression of national consciousness....The consciousness of self
> is not the closing of a door to communication. Philosophic thought teaches us,
> on the contrary, that it is its guarantee....It is at the heart of national conscious-
> ness that international consciousness lives and grows. And this two-fold emerg-
> ing is ultimately only the source of all culture.[29]

Let us briefly summarize the major areas of the agreement of Cabral, Fanon, and Memmi on the connections between colonialism and culture. First, they all believed that the basis of colonialism was material. Second, they recognized that there was a link between politics and culture in a colonial situation. The colonizer was materially bound to culturally repress the colonized, to institutionalize the racism to carry out that repression so that his meanings would be the dominant ones. Third, they discerned that the colonized must know the history of their national culture and the dynamics of its relationship with the cultural repression of the colonizer in order for that national culture to serve as an instrument of resistance. While the views on colonialism of these three intellectuals were not identical — Cabral and Memmi giving some more emphasis to the material basis than Fanon — they were in sufficient accord in these fundamental areas to provide a beginning framework for investigating the internal colonialism which confronts African-Americans. However, before we examine the relationship between American colonization and black culture, we should briefly trace the history of the internal colonialism model and the attendant controversy about its validity.

African-Americans and the Case for Internal Colonialism

In this section of the chapter, we shall analyze some of the disputes regarding the applicability of the internal colonialism model to the

African-American experience, explore the connections between classical colonialism and the African-American past, and suggest a colonial periodization of that past.

In the more than forty years that scholars have explored the internal colonialism model for its applicability to African-Americans, some have rejected the paradigm outright because certain conditions of the African-American experience did not seem congruent with classical colonialism. Among those conditions were the following: 1) there was no separation of land between the colonizing country and African-Americans; 2) African-Americans were not victimized on their own land; 3) African-Americans were in the numerical minority; 4) African-Americans did not constitute a nation; and 5) slavery was not colonialism. Obviously the first three factors are irrefragable, although those scholars who subscribe to the internal colonialism notion argue that 1) those conditions are not the crucial ones, 2) those conditions are compatible with colonialism, or even that 3) those conditions intensify colonialism. Those theorists who support the first two contentions aver that institutional subordination, undergirded by a racist ideology, is the most important factor of colonialism. African-American Marxist historian Jack O'Dell summarizes this view when he posits that "in defining the colonial problem, it is the role of the institutional mechanisms of colonial domination which are decisive."[30] A few theorists, including the author, take the third position as well. Before we establish the historical roots of the internal colonialism idea, let us explore the fourth and fifth conditions that have predisposed some to reject that idea as a way to approach African-American history.

The question of whether or not African-Americans comprise a nation is a perennial one. Obviously, if one defines a nation as a stable, historically developed community of people with a territory, economic life, distinctive culture, and language in common, there has been and is no black nation in this country. However, as African-American historian Rodney Carlisle notes, the idea of a black nation has some objective justification:

> Blacks in America have had not only a separate economic status and a more or less clearly separate ethnic identity, but also a degree of separate culture, separate religious structures, and separate social institutions.[31]

Moreover, as African-American sociologist Alphonso Pinkney indicates, "black nationalist sentiment in the United States can be traced back to the first slave conspiracy in 1526."[32] And then, after the Constitution explicitly endorsed slavery in 1787, free blacks increased organizing around their colonized status in the face of the colonies' new freedom. So, there has always been black nationalist sentiment in this country, and for over two hundred years there have been African-Americans who articulated the view that blacks are a nation within a nation. Although Martin Delany, nineteenth-century African-American historian and physician, appears to have been the first to use the term "nation within a nation" when in 1852 he drew parallels between the Poles in Russia, the Hungarians in Austria, and the Irish, Welsh, and Scotch under British domination and African-Americans, blacks in the late eighteenth century described themselves as belonging to a people with a distinct and inferior status in this country.

Several African-American scholars have recently inferred that this sense of black nationalism derived from being the subject of a colonial situation. Social psychologist Arthur Mathis holds that the "racial struggle must be analyzed in terms of what it is — a colonial conflict. Black nationalism is merely the outgrowth of this conflict."[33] Historian John Bracey, Jr. also suggests a relationship of black nationalism to colonialism when he defines the former:

> Black nationalism as a body of ideas and a pattern of behavior stemming logically from the colonial relationship of Black America to white America is both a response to colonial subordination and an affirmation of the existence off an alternative nationality and set of values.[34]

The critical point is that an unbroken tradition of black nationalism has existed in the United States and is traceable to black struggle against colonialism, including their struggle against a different Weltanschauung.

The argument that slavery was not colonialism is not tenable if one approaches the oppression of African-Americans as part of larger phenomenon. African-American historian Lerone Bennett, Jr., in a significant analysis of internal colonialism in his book *The Shaping of Black America*, shows why such a perspective is necessary for understanding that oppression:

The history of black America is an act in the larger drama of the worldwide colonization of peoples of color by Europeans....Europeans created a colonial system that perpetuated the political, economic and cultural exploitation of non-Europeans.35

White sociologist Robert Blauner, one of the earlier articulators of the internal colonialism model, further develops this point of view:

The common features ultimately relate to the fact that classical colonialism of the imperialist era and American racism both developed out of the same historical situation and reflected a common world economic and power stratification... Because classical colonialism and America's internal colonialism developed out of similar technological, cultural, and power relations, a common process of social oppression characterized the racial patterns in the two contexts.[36]

In sum, African-American psychologist J.H. Howard suggests that those scholars who have rejected the internal colonialism model to explain black oppression have not recognized the larger picture of European organized domination, and so saw slavery as "a relationship between individual slaveholders and slaves...rather than...between metropolitan white society and colonial black society in which the rapid development of the former society"[37] was predicated on the subjugation of the latter. So, as Bennett claims, "the foundations of the (colonial) system were constructed during the slave regime,"[38] which was part and parcel of a larger European pattern.

Now that the five conditions which have caused some critics to deny the validity of the internal colonialism model have been addressed, it will be useful to extend the parallels between classical colonialism and African-American internal colonialism beyond slavery as a prelude to a brief overall periodization of the latter phenomenon. O'Dell, in a very important article, "Colonialism and the Negro American Experience," uses the period of slavery as a point of departure for the internal colonial system and follows that system into the twentieth century. He reminds the reader that the revolution of the thirteen American colonies "left the institution of slavery intact, [which] meant, in effect, that the African population in America remained a colonized people."[39] Continuing to draw parallels between European imperialism and black oppression to demonstrate the common roots, he shows that the same "mechanisms by which Reconstruction was overthrown...compare favorably with what the European colonists...were doing on the African continent during the same periods."[40] He details the mechanisms of internal colonial rule in the last quarter of the nineteenth century and makes a general comparison with the tactics of the Europeans during that time:

> Segregated by law, disfranchised, robbed of its share of wages by discriminatory employment patterns, confronted by a police power and illegal mobs acting in the role of an occupational force, the target of a mass culture of racism and the barbarism of lynching, the Negro American community was imprisoned in a colonial relationship, designed by the new industrial power elite of America, at the very time that the European colonists were partitioning the African continent among themselves.[41]

O'Dell concludes that the African-American experience continues to be one of internal colonialism; in fact, "the status of the black population in the United States is one of the major examples of colonialism in the twentieth century."[42]

One additional critical point needs to be made about the African-American history of internal colonialism; it seems to have developed in three stages, though overlapping ones. The first stage, occurring in slavery, was direct control. Although house slaves and slave drivers did sometimes serve as intermediaries, the system was essentially one of direct control, where either the master or his white plenipotentiary — the small colonizer, i.e., the overseer — held authority.

The second stage, segregated neo-colonialism, began primarily after the Civil War, and was the first phase of indirect control. African-American sociologist Robert Staples, in the seminal article "Race and Colonialism: The Domestic Case in Theory and Practice," asserts that "neocolonialism is a post-emancipation form of colonialism."[43] Bennett appraises the machinations of white capitalistic leaders of Reconstruction:

> While the white leaders of the North and South were building the new system, they were at the same time digging pits for the new stratum of black merchants, teachers, and preachers spawned by the burgeoning network of black schools, churches, businesses, and fraternal institutions. The point...was...simple enough: how to use these emerging leaders in a classical colonial campaign of indirect rule.[44]

These schools, churches, businesses, and fraternal orders were segregated ones, and before the end of the century, the de facto segregation gave way to de jure segregation in the infamous 1896 *Plessy vs. Ferguson* Supreme Court case.

The third stage, integrated neo-colonialism — the second and present phase of indirect control — was fostered in large measure by the equally significant 1954 *Brown vs. Board of Education* Supreme Court case. Again, Bennett deciphers the relationship of that decision to internal colonialism, as he suggests that the result "was another change in the form."[45] This change, which many African-Americans thought would usher in the millennium for them, has had in many ways instead a very deleterious effect. Bennett notes that by the end of the Sixties, "the black colony of America presented... the paradoxical picture of a rapidly growing urban middle section and a rapidly growing reserve army of unemployed and underemployed workers."[46]

The Seventies and early Eighties have witnessed an acceleration of this trend. African-American historian William Strickland sums up the change in African-Americans — especially that rapidly growing middle sector — since Brown when he concludes that "we are individuals in new and unprecedented ways....The race has never before been so fragmented."[47]

Cultural Repression and Education

In the previous section of this chapter, we examined the controversy surrounding the internal colonial model, explored connections between classical colonialism and the African-American past, and pointed up a possible colonial periodization of that past. This section will be an analysis of the general concept of internal colonialism in the African-American experience, some advantages of the internal colonialism model in demystifying that experience, the place of culture in that model, and the role of education in the cultural repression of African-Americans.

Internal colonialism is a form of domestic racist capitalism. In this study, the author submits that one link between race and class in the African-American experience is the status-ordering system. For more than forty-one years, black scholars have employed the concept of a colony to explain the dynamics of African-American life. In 1946, black writer Richard Wright declared that "The Negro is intrinsically a colonial subject, but one who lives not in China, India or Africa but next door to his conquerors, attending their schools, fighting their wars, and laboring in their factories."[48] Since that time, scholars have related internal colonialism to the different aspects — economic, social, political, educational, literary, and psychological — of black life. Black activists — beginning with Malcolm X (El-Hajj Malik El-Shabazz)—have agreed with Wright that "the American Negro problem...is but a facet of the global problem that splits the world in two."[49] For our purposes, it seems more fruitful to identify the possible heuristic advantages of using internal colonialism as an instrument to make a cultural critique of the African-American experience rather than to recount the history of its application. The author suggests the following advantages of the internal colonialism paradigm:

1. Its identification of the common roots of European colonization of African peoples everywhere "makes it possible to use Third World methodologies in deciphering the black experience and formulating developmental strategies."[50]

2. Its identification of the common roots of European colonization of African peoples everywhere makes it possible to demystify the commonality of their present conditions and to understand the objective basis for their unity.

3. Its emphasis on racist/capitalistic institutional domination helps to demystify the different problem areas of black life, including the sense of widening class cleavages among African-Americans. In this study, we shall concentrate on the problems of cultural repression that arise from education. Earlier, we referred to O'Dell's judgement that "in defining the colonial problem, it is the role of the institutional mechanisms of colonial domination which are important."[51]

4. Its emphasis on racist/capitalistic institutional domination assists in demystifying what African-American sociologist James Turner refers to as "the rhetoric of the civil rights struggle, in which so much progress was based on the hope of interracial harmony and unity."[52]

12

5. Its serious attention to the superstructure (laws, culture, politics, etc.) recognizes "it as being a preeminent force in colonial relationships,"[53] and so also conduces to demystification.

6. Its perspective that the culture of the colonized is "a dynamic element in colonized societies"[54] rather than some "Pan-Africanists' tendency to accept it as a given and use it as a basis of group unity"[55] aids in the colonized avoiding a flawed cultural critique of their condition and thus a flawed politics.

7. Its compatibility with the status-ordering system dimension of cultural repression affords the theorist an opportunity to explore that dimension as a possible link in the interaction between race and class. As Staples notes, "to the extent that racial membership is associated with status, we would expect to find some kind of prestige ranking by race-linked phenomena."[56]

Each of these heuristic advantages of the internal colonialism paradigm makes demystification of the African-American experience more likely. Each of them at some level also relates to the culture of the colonized and the cultural repression of the colonizer.

As black sociologist Herman George indicates, culture has been "the single most important topic of theoretical interest, when viewed in relation to the total structure of domination[57] among proponents of internal colonialism. So it is in this analysis. Further, the author agrees with Blauner that "cultural conflict is generic to the colonial relation because colonization involves the domination of Western technological values over the more communal cultures of non-Western peoples,"[58] including African-Americans. Concurring with Fanon, Blauner considers the cultural repression of the colonizer an institutionalized "policy that constrains, trans- forms, or destroys indigenous values, orientations, and ways of life."[59] Staples concludes that "colonial society constructs hierarchies of culture with the Euro-American values occupying a domineering position."[60] African-American scholar of communication, Molefi Asante, suggests that the aim of cultural repression is "cultural dependency and social allegiance of the colonized to the colonizer."[61] If this cultural repression succeeds, Staples projects that it may render the colonized "more vulnerable to certain racial forces."[62] For instance, he says that if blacks abandon the value of communalism, subordination of collective needs to personal desires will undermine "the group's ability to effectively resist the vicissitudes of colonialism."[63]

So as Cabral, Fanon, and Memmi had theorized about the role of cultural repression and the relationship between economics, politics, and culture in the colonial situations with which they were most familiar, these American scholars have also postulated the centrality of cultural repression in the African-American experience of colonialism. This means that the colonized must understand that centrality in order to enlist culture in their resistance. As Cruse insists, a "poor cultural analysis leads...to a flawed and inadequate political response."[64] Let us now turn to education, a critical institution for the maintenance of and the resistance to cultural repression.

Earlier, we noted Memmi's belief that education controlled by the colonizer creates such a permanent duality in the colonized that he/she will not be saved nationally. Several African-American scholars have also identified the role that education assumes in the colonizer's cultural repression. Educator Jomills Braddock asserts that it is "the primary vehicle for achieving cultural dominance."[65] Educator Patti Peterson, realizing that cultural dominance is inherent in colonialism, argues that education "often serves as the vehicle for intellectual aggression. It becomes far more than the transmission of knowledge; it is also the engine of transformation of peoples."[66] Bennett, recognizing that the colonizer must rely on more than physical force to sustain colonialism, claims that the oppressor will also use diametrically opposed methods of force to occupy the minds of the colonized:

> He can forcibly deny the oppressed education, thereby limiting their social and economic possibilities, or he can forcibly educate the oppressed, thereby giving them his values and making them instruments of his purposes.[67]

Bennett warrants that by making the colonized ashamed of themselves and their values (dehumanization), the colonizer intends the "cultural retardation of a whole people and the systematic repression of their values, insights, and expressions."[68] Sociologist Douglas Davidson supports Bennett's idea of dehumanization, suggesting that colonial education is a "tool to perpetuate the colonizer's sense of superiority and to induce a feeling of inferiority in the colonized subjects."[69] Other scholars such as historian Vincent Harding, literary critic/critic Houston Baker, writer Michael Thelwell, psychologist Louis Williams, and educators Preston Wilcox and Michele Russell, as well as those mentioned earlier, subscribe to the notion that education is part and parcel of African-American internal colonialism.

Although education — or the lack of it — has always been a weapon that the colonizer wielded against African-American understanding and thus its humanity, in this study we shall concentrate on the way that education has been employed by the colonizer since the black student movement of the Sixties to create a buffer class among the colonized. The author, who was taught and/or served as an administrator at the college level since 1968, will not provide a history or detailed analysis of those years, but rather adduce some brief insights as to the meaning of that period for the liberation struggle of African-Americans. By liberation struggle, the author means the struggle for freedom from the mystification and dehumanization of this colonial order.

Baker is clear about the subtleness and the devastation of the American educational system. Branding it "a bastion of racism...striving desperately to maintain the status quo...(in which) white America has spent billions of dollars and a great amount of repressive energy to insure the dominance of white meanings,"[70] he summarizes the general impact of the white college and university welcome to black students:

> The ways of colonialism are subtle indeed. To draw off the young, to place them in institutions that alienate them from their culture has a devastating impact on the growth of any nation. And the type of literacy guaranteed by the academy today is still not calculated to provide anything approaching an adequate definition of black life in America....The majority of black students...seldom...come...to any sense of themselves as representatives of a unique culture.[71]

Turner and black historian W. Eric Perkins elaborate further on the phenomena of mystification and dehumanization which proceed from the training that black students receive in bourgeois institutions, which have as their ultimate purpose the defense and authentication of the American racist/capitalistic/sexist society and Euro-American culture:

> To date, the Afro-American intelligentsia has been deficient in uncovering the 'reality' behind 'the appearance,' leaving our self-understanding and the politics associated with coming to self-consciousness in a vacuum.[72]

As Braddock notes, these "native elites...are unable to move affirmatively toward liberation because of their failing to recognize their own oppression."[73]

Turner explains that the increased number of black students in white universities proceeded from an effort "to create greater acceptance of the social system by giving them a vested interest in its benefits,"[74] not because it was the moral thing to do or that America had no choice but to accede to black student demands for larger admissions. Thus, the real purpose behind the newly opened doors was to produce "a large national black bourgeoisie as a stabilizing social class to counteract the growing alienation and disruptive currents among the black masses."[75]

According to Turner and Perkins, this attempt of the colonizer to preempt the black student movement and appropriate young black intellectuals has been alarmingly successful. As a consequence of the bourgeois social, economic, and political theory they absorb, "integrationism, black capitalism, the success myth, (and) possessive individualism are results of such ideological domination and manipulation."[76] They point out that thus the social outlook of these students "is social reformism; the philosophy of economic and property acquisition, personal thrift and moral righteousness."[77] Finally, they raise a sensitive but crucial issue in the demystification of the African-American colonial experience when they maintain that the cultural nationalism of that period was in some ways reactionary because it "was not antithetical to this view, since it did not foster an anti-capitalist position."[78] The upshot of this substantial colonial success has been aptly described by Baker:

> Articulate young blacks who might have played significant roles in the black community have been effectively removed. Their training in the academy makes it unlikely that they will ever return home.[79]

Must African-Americans accept such co-optation of its own young? The author thinks not. blacks must develop a strategy of institutionalized resistance to the mystification and dehumanization inherent in this colonial educational system. First, blacks who are in educational institutions — and/or who are parents of the young — must follow the counsel of Turner and Perkins and promote their own demystification:

We must accept our responsibility to understand the reality of our national oppression, and how various forms of political, economic and social forces intersect to dominate black people as a systematic process of the social order.[80]

Second, those black educators and parents who have demystified their experience of internal colonialism and have reclaimed their own humanity must focus on the cultural duality of their students/children, and in the words of psychologist Louis Williams, "assist them in developing an awareness of the forces of racism and colonialism with its psychological, sociological, and physical oppression."[81] In fact, psychologist Arthur Mathis suggests that it is more important for educators and parents to help black students demystify their experience by teaching "them the true function of the American system...than teaching them racial pride and identity."[82] Is demystification of the American ethos more important than understanding one's identity? Perhaps, rather, the processes are interactive, for one's identity is impacted by the American ethos even as that identity affects one's own ethos. In sum, Turner contends that African-Americans who are concerned with black education "cannot be apolitical because as an internal colony our people are engulfed by the oppressors' institutions."[83] Further, he argues convincingly "that control over content and definition of the learning of our young is a pivotal facet of the liberation struggle."[84]

II

Colonial and African-American
Literary Analyses: Connections

In this chapter, the author will use the province of colonial literature
suggested by Cabral, Fanon, and Memmi as a context for locating a role
that literature can play in the classroom in demystifying the African-
American experience of internal colonialism and contributing to black
student resistance to dehumanization. He will also employ revolutionary
educator Paulo Freire's idea of "generative themes" as one dimension of
a pedagogical literary criticism model that is designed to conduce to those
same two purposes. The chapter is not intended to provide a history of
African-American literature or criticism, or to address the historical con-
troversies regarding the function of that literature/criticism. Rather, the
author will incorporate notions about the history and function of African-
American literature and criticism only as they relate to the model.

Although Fanon is usually discussed when scholars consider colonial
literature, Cabral and Memmi have also articulated the place of literature
in a struggle against colonialism. Even with Fanon, the focus is normally
on his three-stage procession of colonized literature: 1) the "unqualified
assimilation" stage, 2) the "just-before-the-battle" stage of a "borrowed
estheticism," and 3) the "fighting phase."[1] In this section of the chapter,
we shall concentrate on the contribution that Fanon, Cabral, and Memmi
thought literature could make to resistance of the colonizers' cultural
repression and the related tradition of African-American literature and
literary criticism.

An infrequently quoted passage of Fanon serves as a milieu for the
analysis. He determined that literature's "sole really contemporary task...
is to persuade the group to progress to reflection and mediation."[2] This
statement epitomizes the purpose of this literary criticism paradigm: to be
a means which African-American instructors of literature can use to en-

courage the young intellectuals of their nation to seriously deliberate their history, helping them to mediate that history through the study of their literature. Cabral acknowledged a similar function of literature for the colonized intellectual. Although he realized that "the middle-class minority engaged in the pre-independence movement...only occasionally manages to influence the masses" [3] with their writing, he insisted that this does not negate the value of that literature to the struggle:

> It can...influence a sector of the uprooted or those who are latecomers to its own class and an important sector of public opinion..., notably the class of intellectuals.[4]

Memmi also conceded the ambivalence of the colonized writer, but deemed the literature "part of the development of the self-consciousness of an entire human group."[5] He felt that the artist hastened that collective consciousness by participating in it.

Fanon not only understood the cultural duality of the colonized writer, but illustrated how the literature could make an optimum contribution to liberation. Decrying the artist who turned "paradoxically toward the past and away from actual events"[6] of his/her nation, reveling in the glorious and innocent yesteryears, embracing "the castoffs of thought, its shells and corpses, a knowledge which has been stabilized once and after all,"[7] Fanon urged that artist to "realize that the truths of a nation are in the first place its realities."[8] He suggested what the writer must then do:

> He must go on until he has found the seething pot out of which the learning of the future will emerge....The colonized man who writes for his people ought to use the past with the intention of opening the future, as an invitation to action and a basis for hope.[9]

Fanon believed that it was possible and necessary to write literature which was "a true invitation to thought, to demystification, and to battle."[10] He thought that literature could have "unquestioned pedagogical value"[11] when it was "clear...a precise, forward-looking exposition,"[12] when the undertaking of it was "not merely an intellectual advance, but a political advance."[13] Fanon felt that literature could help "to understand the part one has played, to recognize one's advance, and to furbish up one's weapons."[14] And so, we are back to Fanon's conviction, which was mentioned earlier. Literature should "persuade the group to reflection and mediation."[15]

Two related ideas emerge from this analysis of Cabral, Fanon, and Memmi, which serve as a framework for a brief view of African-American literature and criticism. All three theoreticians determined that the literature of colonized intellectuals should be written for the group — with perhaps the petite bourgeoisie benefitting more than the masses — and that such literature was capable of raising the consciousness of the group, hopefully to the level of battle. They rejected an art for art's sake orientation in colonial societies. Fanon thought that literature at its best could persuade the colonized to reflection, demystification, mediation, and maybe even confrontation. Cabral believed that the writing of the colonized middle-class minority could have substantial impact on a certain group — the petite bourgeoisie — and as such would constitute a valuable asset to the colonial struggle. Literature could influence the uprooted, the class of intellectuals. Memmi felt that the literature of the colonized writer not only reflected a developing self-consciousness of the group, but also would accelerate the collective consciusness of the group. In sum, according to Cabral, Fanon and Memmi, the literature of colonized intellectuals could contribute to both demystification and resistance to dehumanization, including their own.

African-Americans have such a tradition of collective and consciousness-raising literature. Although generally it was not addressed specifically to Blacks until the middle '60s, its central impulse, according to white literary critic Keneth Kinnamon, "has been one of collective protest against racism and collective affirmation of black values."[16] Black critics agree with this overall assessment. David Dorsey asserts that "black literature and music have, in every period...been dominated by...the most emotion-laden communal experiences."[17] Donald Gibson, focusing on the depiction of the northern urban experience, suggests that black writers have been preoccupied with the group need of establishing a positive social identity in that situation. He avers that the "tension manifested in the pull at once toward our historical communal values and toward the individualism encouraged by the larger community, underlies most writing by black authors."[18]

Kinnamon, singling out the period of black literary nationalism in the middle and late '60s and early '70s, recognizes that the literature continued to be collective, but that it no longer was addressed principally to

Whites. Further, the primary purpose in writing for an African-American audience was to help demystify their experience. Kinnamon summarizes what he considers the best writing of that period:

> (It) is a serious, sustained...effort to possess imaginatively and to project emotive-ly and intelligibly the collective experience of black people in America and the world in its historical and political as well as personal dimensions. The ultimate purpose of such an artistic activity...is to alter and intensify consciousness, devel-op attitudes, and so lead to action that will ameliorate the worldly and spiritual condition of the people out of whose experience it comes.[19]

Some critics maintain that black literary criticism also possesses a collective and consciousness-raising tradition. Eugenia Collier, probably the first African-American to locate colonial theories at the center of her critical activities, makes the point in her dissertation, "Steps Toward a Black Aesthetic: A Study of Black American Criticism." First, appraising the work of early critics up to 1930, she alleges that they began the collective tradition:

> Early Black American critics...conceived of art as being functional and collective. Even those who consciously minimized social function ('propaganda') envisioned art as a means of being accepted by the white world, a way of improving the lot of the Black community, or at least the part of that community which they consid-ered important....To the black critic, then, art has a deep and lasting commitment to the welfare of the community.[20]

Second, analyzing those same critics, she argues for a tradition of con-sciousness raising with black and white audiences:

> The area in which all critics most emphatically agreed was the concept that litera-ture must be moral....And here the Black critics went far beyond the puritan no-tion of individual morality....Rather, for the black critics, literature had no less a task than the quest for justice and for redress. He was out to salvage the humanity not only of Blacks whom the oppressive system sought to dehumanize, but also of those whites whose ingrained racism was a constant threat to their own human im-pulses. Literature was a means of ascertaining Truth, and this Truth would make both races free.[21]

22

Collier suggests then that although the collectivity and consciousness raising included Whites, the tradition has existed from the beginning of African-American literary criticism.

In 1937, Richard Wright published his "Blueprint for Negro Writing" in the Leftist journal, *New Challenge*, and emphasized the place of collectivity and consciousness raising in black writing. Although a communist at that juncture of his career, Wright understood the need for a nationalist sense among African-American writers — the need to "possess and understand it"[22] — even as they moved to transcend it. Decrying the isolation among black writers and "their lack of a clear realization among themselves of their possible (collective) roles"[23] in relating to the masses of their people, he stresses collectivity regarding social consciousness and responsibility, perspective, and theme. First, because Wright believed that African-American leaders were becoming increasingly bourgeois, he exhorts black writers to assume the serious responsibility of using their work to raise the consciousness of black people, "to do no less than create values by which his race is to struggle, live, and die."[24] Second, Wright maintains that perspective, "that fixed point in intellectual space where a writer stands to view the struggles, hopes, and sufferings of his people,"[25] will come to black writers only "when they have looked and brooded so hard and long upon the harsh lot of their race and compared it with the hopes and struggles of minority peoples everywhere that the cold facts have begun to tell them something." [26] Finally, Wright suggests that theme for black writers "will emerge when they have begun to feel the meaning of the history of their race as though they in one lifetime had lived it themselves throughout all the long centuries." [27]

Kinnamon examines later critics in the '60s and early '70s who were associated with the Black Aesthetic, and explains their perspective regarding the collective and consciousness-raising tradition:

> The whole process of literary creation and consumption should serve the purpose of developing the black collective consciousness and building the black nation rather than adhering to what are considered narrow, individualistic, elitist, or racist standards of beauty.[28]

The black aestheticians certainly sustained the tradition of collectivity and consciousness raising, but they directed their attention to Blacks. Maulana Karenga, one of the most prominent though controversial advocates of the Black Aesthetic, suggests that one of the criteria by which a work of art should be judged is whether or not it is collective. Karenga believes that art, "everyday life given more form and color,...must be from the people and returned to the people,...(and that) an artist may have any freedom to do what he wishes as long as he does not take the freedom from the people to be protected from those images, words and sounds that are negative to their lives and development."[29] Addison Gayle, Jr., another noted proponent of the Black Aesthetic, reinforces Karenga's position on collectivity by asserting that art should "attempt, in Malreaux's phrase, 'to bring man back into the community of man'."[30] Here man is black, Memmi's colonized person, whose "most serious blow... is being removed from history and from the community."[31] In Gayle's "Blueprint for Black Criticism," he adds that art must "inculcate the values of communality between one Black person and another...(and that it) must be in continual revolt against the American attempt to dehumanize man."[32]

Two black critics, after surveying the entire history of African-American literary criticism, show how that history embodies the collective and consciousness-raising tradition. Carol Elder, in her dissertation, "'The Discovery of America': Literary Nationalism in the Criticism of Black American Literature," describes the role which African-American critics "most frequently outline for themselves as one in which all the strengths and weakness of their autobiographical-communal situation must be faced and accounted for."[33] She suggests that they see their most important relationship to a work of art "as a subjective one in which their function is to point out the external relationships between the work of art and the lives of the people it touches."[34] Carolyn Fowler Gerald, taking a somewhat different angle on the tradition, employs the term demystification to summarize it:

> For because of its preoccupation with stereotypes, authenticity, representatives and even the role of propaganda, black criticism emerges as a tradition of demystification. And that is its most distinctive quality.[35]

Now that the author has provided a framework of the collective and consciousness-raising purposes of literature in a colonial situation — as delineated by Cabral, Fanon, and Memmi — and has illustrated how the history of African-American literature and literary criticism can be read as consonant with those purposes, let us turn to considerations of the model of pedagogical literary criticism, which are consistent with those purposes and that history.

Five theoretical considerations which emerged from our earlier discussion relate to the nature of the critical model subsequently outlined:

1) Cultural repression is inherent in colonialism because it is necessary for the colonizer's continued domination.

2) One of the most effective control agents of cultural repression is the institution of education.

3) The cultural repression dimensions of colonial education are the mystification of the colonial experience and the concomitant dehumanization.

4) The colonized must institutionally assess their national culture and preserve, reclaim, and reproduce elements of that culture which make for a viable configuration to resist their cultural repression.

5) Literature and literary criticism have been used by the colonized for their national purposes of demystification and resistance to dehumanization.

Three other related theoretical considerations impinge upon our model. First, as Gibson aptly points out, "all critical schemes have their basis in values antecedent to literary considerations."[36] The question then seems not whether or not a critical approach is political but whose politics it represents. Critics need to know the value implications of the critical frame of reference from which they proceed. Second, as black literary critic Jerry Ward made clear when discussing the contributions of the Black Aesthetic, "the yoking of social and literary facts is an inextricable part of the process of reading."[37] Third, the author agrees with Ward that beyond the Black Aesthetic, "the new frontier for black criticism is inquiry about the consciousness Afro-American literature makes possible and why."[38]

One other consideration is in order before the critical model is sketched: the precedent for the model. Although, as was mentioned before in the chapter, Collier appears to be the first African-American critic to place colonial theories of cultural repression and resistance at the center of her work, black writer/critic Mari Evans provided the earliest tracings of a critical model based on these theories which should be employed by the classroom instructor to combat that repression. Evan's position is that if literature can be used in effecting cultural repression, then it can "be utilized as an effective, accessible and natural counteractive in the demystifying process."[39] She agrees with poet/novelist Linda Brown Bragg that black survival should motivate African-American writers. The resulting literature should "delineate the tenuous and regressive nature of our rela-tionship (as an unorganized directionless nation within a nation) to the U.S."[40] Further, she believes that "fundamental...to the forging of critical tools with which to explore the literature of an oppressed people is a basic understanding of the relationship they have to the society that assaults them."[41] That relationship, Evans insists, is a colonial one. At the heart of her critical design is the following segment (edited by the author) of an unpublished paper delivered on April 23, 1983, at the UCLA Center for Afro-American Studies Spring Symposium:

> Reflections of the dynamics of any oppressive...system will be endemic to the literature of the target population and can be identified as motifs or statements, whether or not deliberately structured of the activities and behavior of a colonized people and may be interpreted variously, but not exclusively as:
>
>> 1) Manifestations of forms of conflict which owe their uniqueness to the specificity of the Black experience, e.g. self-hatred....2) Prototypical struggles of the people to free themselves from colonization....3) Statement of emotional or intellectual metamorphosis: or acquiescence to, or triumph over the...pervasive control; 4) Exploration of selected areas of impingement e.g., the effects of colonization.[42]

Evans emphasizes "the need for a critical classroom approach that is initially sociopolitical, one that finds examining the nature and methodology of colonization imperative to the study and exploration of African-American literature."[43] She also suggests that "supplementary materials of a historical, statistical, theoretical, or generally nonfictional nature can be introduced as related reading."[44]

The author was introduced to this literary criticism model in a private interview at the home of Evans during the 1983 Kwanzaa holiday week. He was amazed by the congruence of certain parts of her model with the one that he was structuring. Admittedly, her scheme influenced the author's thinking, although the configuration of his paradigm has assumed a different shape. The following discussion is a description of that paradigm, which the author labels metaphorical and metamorphical literary criticism. The author suggests neither this model represents the only approach that instructors of African-American literature may use to assist black students in demystifying their experience nor certainly that it represents all that instructors should consider when approaching that literature. It is therefore projected as an alternative and partial approach to the study of African-American literature. Although the author shares Ward's concern that "in our educational systems black students are baptized with (critical) norms that may be incorrect,"[45] he recognizes, along with Houston Baker, that "the function of the pedagogue or teacher in the classroom is finally to teach one's own values through the agency of works of art."[46] Finally, although the author recognizes the limitations of literature and education — as parts of the superstructure — to affect the base, a colonial analysis or deconstruction of African-American literature can be employed to make more lucid to black students the relationship of the superstructure to the base. Thus, the purposes of this model are to enhance the ability of black students to make an adequate cultural critique of their historical experience, to establish or reestablish continuity with their culture, and to understand their own cultural duality.

Metaphorical and Metamorphical Literary Criticism

At the core of this pedagogical literary criticism paradigm is the use of what Paulo Freire brands "generative themes" to illustrate the metaphorical relationship of each African-American to all others (the author calls this intensive universality); to illustrate the metamorphosis of black self-portrayals, characterizations, and poetic individuations toward myth — or the lack thereof; and/or to reflect the mythic qualities of black self-portrayals, characterizations, and poetic individuations in order to explore questions about the derivative themes of identity and ethos which may contribute to a metamorphosis in black student consciousness. By mythic qualities, the author means qualities central to those self-portrayals, characterizations, and poetic individuations who demystify their colonial realities, reproducing the myths of black identity and black ethos. It is important that questions be raised about the "saturation" (to borrow African-American literary critic Stephen Henderson's term) of the literary treatment of those derivative themes. By "saturation," the author means themes which reflect "a sense of fidelity to the observed and intuited truth of the Black experience." [47] This fidelity or lack thereof can be investigated in dialogue between instructor and students, using the historical readings suggested in the appendix and their own experiences as bases for the reasoned or felt conclusions. To better understand how this model works, the author will discuss its five major dimensions: 1) generative themes, 2) intensive universality, 3) metamorphical event and metamorphical intent, 4) dialectic of chronological and colonial historicity, and 5) intertextuality.

As mentioned above, the use of generative themes in classroom dialogue between instructor and students to raise the level of critical consciousness is usually attributed to Freire. Amplifying the definition of generative themes provided in the introduction, the author returns to Freire's relating that concept to the concepts of an epoch and the thematic universe:

> An epoch is characterized by a complex of ideas, concepts, hopes, doubts, values, and challenges in dialectical interaction with their opposites, striving toward plenitude. The concrete representation of many of these ideas, values, concepts, and hopes, as well as the obstacles which impede man's hopes, as well as the obstacles which impede mans's full humanization, constitute the themes of that epoch. These themes imply others which are opposing or even antithetical....The complex of interacting themes of an epoch constitutes its thematic universe. [48]

The author agrees with Freire that "the broadest epochal unit...contains themes of a universal character (and that) the fundamental theme of our epoch (is)...domination — which implies its opposite, the theme of liberation." [49] However, since "generative themes can be located in concentric circles, moving from the general to the particular," [50] he suggests that the fundamental general theme for people of African descent all over the world is colonization — an historical form of European domination —

with its opposite being decolonization. Colonization gives rise to many particular generative themes, but this literary criticism model, through textual and intertextual analysis, focuses on those of mystification and dehumanization and their opposites, especially on the derivative themes of colonial identity and ethos and their opposites. Out of the tension between the colonial derivative themes and their opposites arose what the author terms the archetypal pattern of cultural duality and the myths of black identity and ethos.

Intensive universality is the idea that all African-Americans — even if they escape the worst physical and economic ravages of America's racist/capitalistic/sexist society — are subjected to the colonial themes of mystification and dehumanization. Wright said that the Negro is America's metaphor; this author asserts that each African-American is a metaphor for all Blacks, in that cultural duality has always been and continues to be shared by all Blacks. Only the forms of mystification and dehumanization have changed; the attack on African-American understanding of their historical condition and the related attack on their identity and ethos have been generic to the black experience. Metaphorical analysis raises questions about the intensive universality of that cultural duality through a textual or intertextual examination of the relationship of mystification and dehumanization generative themes and their derivative themes of European-American identity and ethos to the self-portrayals in black autobiographies, the chracterizations in black novels, and to the poetic individuations in black narrative poetry.

Metamorphical event and metamorphical intent are the two related factors involved in metamorphical analysis. Metamorphical event refers to the textual appropriation (re-reading) or reflection of the generative themes in self-portrayals, characterizations, and the poetic individuations to explore the event of metamorphosis in the autobiographer, fiction characters, and poet/poetic individuations. By event, the author means the evolving fact of metamorphosis and not an isolated incident contributing to it. Metamorphical intent refers to the author's aims in constructing the paradigm: to help African-American students to reconstruct memory, to understand their cultural duality, and to make an adequate cultural critique of the black experience. Metamorphical intent includes the investigation of the inherency of generative themes and their derivative themes in African-American literature and the use of metamorphical event as well as mythic self-portrayals, characterizations, and poetic individuations to examine the intensive universality of the black experience in order to conduce to the metamorphosis of black students. It also includes inquiring about the writer's metamorphical intent.

Both the metaphorical and metamorphical analyses require historical context for the setting/work or what the author terms the dialectic of chronological and colonial historicity. In this model, the chronological part of this dynamic will be an examination of historical interpretations of the historical period(s) — slavery, segregated neo-colonialism, and integrated neo-colonialism — of the setting/work. The colonial part of the dynamic will be based on historical analyses of the changing institutional forms of cultural repression and an intertextual analysis of the changing forms as evidenced in the literature. In the appendix, the author has provided the instructor a five-part list of references which puts each of those historical periods in the context of the entire history of African-Americans. They include 1) general histories 2) the three period histories, and 3) analyses which focus on the dialectic of chronological/colonial historicity. It is incumbent upon the instructor to engender questions regarding the inherent tension between the passage of actual time and the stasis of colonial time — the persisting present — in the dialectic of chronological/colonial historicity.

As we have seen in the discussion of the first four major dimensions, intertextuality comes into play in the analysis of the persistence of the generative themes of mystification and dehumanization and their derivative themes as well as their opposites; in the investigation of the intensive universality of the African-American experience; in the examination of mythic self-portrayals, characterizations, and poetic individuations and/or their metamorphosis; and in the exploration of colonial historicity. As this model is applied in chapters three through eight, most of the inter-textual analysis will necessarily occur in the conclusion, where there is the perusal of all the texts in their respective historical periods. However, some intertextual analysis will take place in those chapters where there is more than one text involved.

III

Douglass' "Power of Truth" Against "Irresponsible Power"

Even though the harsh fugitive slave law of the Compromise of 1850, the Kansas-Nebraska Act of 1854, and the Dred Scott decision of 1857 — all of which reflected the tenor of the times — contributed to Frederick Douglass' most militant positions, when he supported at times the ideas of slave violence and emigration of free African-Americans during that tempestuous decade, the *Narrative of the Life of Frederick Douglass, an American Slave* presaged such developments. Published in 1845, the *Narrative* illustrated a personality who not only was repulsed by the physical atrocities of slavery, but who also understood and resisted the cultural assault of that form of colonialism. Identification with the slavemaster was the supreme assault, and Douglass showed how this was effected, even how he was threatened. More important though, he pointed out how he escaped this psychological association. In order to understand Douglass' analysis of how it was possible for slavery to result in such mystification and dehumanization for the slaves that it was possible for them to partially identify with their owners and how he was able to ground his own identity in experiential communality, we need to use Douglass' notions of the "power of truth" and "irresponsible power" [1] as the philosophical context to examine slave feelings about "kind" slavemasters and other "kind" whites. We shall emphasize the experiences of Douglass, including the meaning of physical resistance to Douglass' identity, and his relationships with slaves and free blacks. It will be argued that the "irresponsible power" of the slaveowners in the *Narrative* without the "power of truth" of slaves demystifying their servitude contributed to slave individualism and thus in part to their identification with their slavemasters. Conversely, that "power of truth," even

31

in the presence of "irresponsible power," encouraged communalism and thus slave identification with each other. This became Douglass' freedom before his physical liberation and increased his sensibilities for slaves and free African-Americans afterward.

Douglass suggested that the "power of truth" and "irresponsible power" provided a framework to analyze the effects of slavery on slaveowners as well as slaves. Ironically, it was one of his slavemasters, Hugh Auld, who was responsible for Douglass' moment of truth. Auld, discovering that his wife, Sophia, had been teaching Douglass to read, not only forced her to abandon the practice, but also informed her that education would break the chains of bondage that had been loosened by the slaves' instinctive understanding that they should be free and their visceral opposition to slavery in spite of efforts to dehumanize them:

> A nigger should know nothing but to obey his master — to do as he is told to do. Learning would spoil the best nigger in the world. Now,...if you teach that nigger... how to read, there would be no keeping him. It would ever unfit him to be a slave. He would at once become unmanageable, and of no value to his master.[2]

This "new and special revelation, explaining dark and mysterious things," [3] was the key to what Douglass called "a most perplexing difficulty — to wit, the white man's power to enslave the black man." [4] He added that "from that moment, I understood the pathway from slavery to freedom."[5]

This awareness of the importance of education — not necessarily formal, but the power of reading and reason — became the "power of truth" in Douglass' life; and after he read a dialogue in *The Columbian Orator* between a master and his slave, and one of Sheridan's speeches on Catholic emancipation, he admits new sentiments about slaveowners:

> The more I read, the more I was led to abhor and detest my enslavers. I could regard them in no other light than a band of successful robbers, who had left their homes, and gone to Africa, and stolen us from our homes, and in a strange land reduced us to slavery. I loathed them as being the meanest as well as the most wicked of men.[6]

Not only did the "power of truth" make it possible for Douglass to hate slaveowners, but it made it impossible for him to identify with even the "kindest" of them. He came to believe that "irresponsible power" accounted for their inhumane behavior, and so regarded Sophia Auld's change of heart in not only ceasing his instruction in reading but becoming "even more violent in her opposition than her husband himself." [7] He also attributed the subsequent inhumanity of the slave auction of which he was a part and the actions of a later master, Thomas Auld, to this power.

Douglass inferred that the "irresponsible power" of slavemasters without the slaves having the "power of truth" perpetuated the system of slavery. Thus, near the end of the *Narrative*, he recounts how Thomas Auld attempted to secure his enslavement:

> He exhorted me to content myself, and be obedient. He told me, if I would be
> happy, I must lay out no plans for the future. He said, if I behaved myself properly, he would take care of me. Indeed, he advised me to complete thoughtlessness
> of the future, and taught me to depend solely upon him for happiness. He seemed
> to see fully the pressing necessity of setting aside my intellectual nature, in order
> to contentment in slavery. [8]

Earlier, Douglass explained how the slavebreaker, Edward Covey, had transformed him into a "brute" even in the face of his ability to read, by forcing him to concentrate all his energies on survival. Douglass remembered that his "intellect languished, (and) the disposition to read departed." [9] Even in milder circumstances, he emphasized the frustration of education affording "a view of my wretched condition, without the remedy." [10] Douglass believed that although the "power of truth" would liberate the slave psychologically, the "irresponsible power" of the slaveowner might set in a despair so shocking that the truth would not set him/her free. So it was necessary for the slave to both understand his/her condition and to be able to forge at least a psychological way out of it. This was often accomplished by the communalism that derived from Africa and was reinforced by slave identification with other slaves. In sum, Douglass felt that the "power of truth" would enhance such slave identification and minimize slave identification with slavemasters.

Now that the framework is established, let us consider Douglass' analysis of the scheme of mystification that slavemasters used to augment their physical "irresponsible power:" keep the "power of truth" from the slaves, and thus encourage slave identification with them. Douglass summarizes the slavemasters' strategy:

I have found that, to make a contented slave, it is necessary to make a thoughtless one. It is necessary to darken his moral and mental vision, and, as far as possible, to annihilate the power of reason. He must be able to detect no inconsistencies in slavery; he must be made to feel slavery is right.[11]

In the *Narrative*, the slaveowners tried to undermine the "power of truth" by being "kind," conferring privileges and glutting the slave with freedom. Being "kind" ranged from giving permission for a slave not to be in the field at sunrise to less flagrant policies of physical violence and food denial. The latter policies were said to be particularly true in the cities, due to the peer pressure of non-slaveholding neighbors.

Kindness was supposed to demonstrate the slavemaster's humanity, to soften the contradiction of his holding slaves as chattel; nevertheless, when he gave special permission excusing a slave from "can't see to can't see" labor, Douglass said that the master touted the privilege. The outstanding act of beneficence was selecting slaves "to do errands at the Great House Farm,"[12] the home plantation of Colonel Lloyd. It was designed to show the slaves that they were worthy of great confidence, bolstering their besieged egos.

Glutting the slaves with freedom was cited in cases of slaves stealing molasses, when "asking for more food than their regular allowance,"[13] and on holidays. When slaves stole molasses, they were forced to eat until nauseated. When asking for additional food, they were whipped for being hard to please if they were unable to consume gargantuan portions in a set amount of time. Douglass spent more time, however, in discussing the scheme of slaveowners allowing the days between Christmas and New Year's day as holidays to provide an outlet for slaves' frustration. This stratagem for getting slaves to forget their bondage, Douglass claimed, was "part and parcel of the gross fraud, wrong, and inhumanity of slavery,"[14] and was "among the most effective means in the hands of the slaveholder in keeping down the spirit of insurrection."[15] He pointed out that the slaveholders'" object seems to be, to disgust their slaves with freedom by plunging them into the lowest depths of dissipation...to disgust the slave with freedom, by allowing him to see only the abuse of it...so that many of us were led to think that there was little to choose between liberty and slavery."[16] The slaves, jaded with drunkenness and frolicking, would return to the fields, "feeling, upon the whole, rather glad to go, from what our master had deceived us into a belief was freedom, back to the arms of slavery."[17] Douglass thought that this gross fraud was possible because most slaves were ill-equipped with the "power of truth." It could be inferred that it was also useful in promoting slave identification with masters. Whether the identification that grew out of these subterfuges derived from an illusion of shared interests, the need to patch frail egos, or the emergence of the ostensible first law of nature, such identification assuredly worked at cross-purposes with slave communalism.

Some textual evidence in the *Narrative* suggests that at least partial slave identification with slavemasters did exist. Although we cannot necessarily ascribe such identification to slaves claiming that they possessed "kind" masters — whether for survival reasons or because their masters seemed less cruel than others — the arguments among themselves about who had the best master as well as Douglass' insights into slave feelings regarding the privileges of getting to see Baltimore or being sent to the Great House Farm do suggest partial mystification and association with the slavemasters.

The phenomenon of slaves quarreling "among themselves about the relative goodness of their masters, each contending for the superior goodness of his own over that of the others"[18] is one with mixed implications for identification. Even though they would "mutually execrate their masters when viewed separately,"[19] one has to account for the slaves vaunting the wealth, intelligence and manliness of their respective masters to the point of fisticuffs. Why would they "think that the greatness of their master was transferable to themselves,"[20] and that the supreme disgrace was "to be a poor man's slave?"[21] Douglass believed that those slaves were without the "power of truth." It seems, thus, that the lack of this power in a society that was increasingly emphasizing the individual contributed to a compelling need to shore up one's identity, to be a part of power. Even if that support issued from identification with masters, and set them at loggerheads with other slaves, those tensions were endured, for it became more tolerable to deem someone beneath you than to admit there was only one rung for a slave — the bottom one.

This ratiocination may also pertain to the self-esteem of some of Colonel Lloyd's slaves and the high valuation accorded them by others when they were "selected to do errands at the Great House Farm...(or) allowed to see Baltimore."[22] Although in the case of self-esteem, one must admit that part of the honor of the mission was being out of the fields and away from the lash, and that Douglass hinted that they were not above fawning to secure the favor of the overseers, yet "it was associated in their minds with greatness."[23] There was no interplantation rivalry as in the illustration above, but perpetual competition obtained among Lloyd's slaves, and "he was called the smartest and most trusty fellow, who had this honor conferred upon him the most frequently."[24] Douglass' subsequent discussion of the songs that the chosen ones sang on the way to the farm with "at once the highest joy and deepest sadness"[25] reflected the tension between the hunger for identity and the passion for freedom. Douglass drew a comparison between them and "a man cast away upon a desolate island,"[26] suggesting that they were born without the "power of truth" and the power to get to the mainland of liberty. In the case of slave status, the four Blacks who helped to man Lloyd's large sloop were no doubt "looked upon as the privileged ones of the plantation,"[27] in part because sailing to market at Baltimore temporarily lifted the yoke of thralldom. Baltimore, for some, may have seemed halfway to freedom, with its apparent ease of constraints for city slaves. Still, especially for those without the "power of truth," the longing of the marked for a mark must have been at work, although finally it was to be registered in another name.

There was one reference to slaves regarding an overseer "kind." On the farm of Captain Anthony, Douglass' first master, the slaves determined Mr. Hopkins to be a "good overseer" because he was less cruel than the previous overseer and took no pleasure when he did whip them. This sentiment seems to reflect self-identification.

There was also only one report of slave feelings about other "kind" whites. The slaves of Thomas Auld — Douglass included — were fond of Reverend George Cookman. They thought that Cookman had influenced a rich slaveholder to free his slaves and "that he was laboring to effect the emancipation of all the slaves."[28] They believed that he "took more notice of us than either of the other ministers,"[29] and deduced that he was sympathetic to their plight. Certainly, this "love" of the slaves was not identification with their masters, but with themselves.

Douglass' identification with "kind" slaveowners seems negligible, even though his experiences with them and their families were several. Although Douglass mentioned some of the lavish possessions of Colonial Lloyd and even as a boy had tried to impress upon his cousin, Tom, the

grandeur of the Great House, we find no instances of such possible identification with his masters after he discovered the "power of truth."

Douglass was either a slave to or lived with five different "masters,"
their families and overseers. Of these, he only labelled three, at any time,
"kind." He said that he judged a master to be kind if he measured up to
or surpassed the standards of kindness set up by other masters in the area.
Although he alluded that his first master, Captain Anthony, seldom
whipped him; that Anthony's son, Daniel, protected him from the older
boys and shared his cakes; and that he agreed with the other slaves' estimate that Hopkins was a good overseer; most of his references to "kind"
masters related to the Hugh Auld family and Mr. Freeland. Hugh Auld
and his wife, Sophia, assumed a prominent place in the *Narrative* of
Douglass. When introduced to them, he was struck by Sophia's "white
face beaming with the most kindly emotions."[30] This had no precedence
in his young life. Nor was he to be disappointed with her early behavior,
for her warmth put Douglass at ease. In fact, she seemed to be troubled
when he addressed her with "crouching servility, usually so acceptable a
quality in a slave."[31] Moreover, she began to teach him to read shortly
after his arrival. All went well until her husband discovered her instruction, and even then, she did not stop immediately. Douglass, later harking
back to her initial kindness and Hugh Auld's disinclination to whip him,
thought that "few slaves could boast of a kinder master and mistress than
myself."[32] Although their conduct subsequently changed, due to Sophia
Auld's anger when suspecting Douglass was pursuing his reading and
Master Auld's drinking, they seemed to have mended their ways in part
when he was returned to them by Thomas Auld, Hugh's brother, after his
attempted escape from Freeland. Once, after Douglass was brutally
beaten by four white apprentice caulkers, they demonstrated their concern for him. She attended his wounds, and Hugh Auld refused to let him
go back to where he had been attacked. After they had restored him to
health, he secured Douglass a job where he was foreman. However, in
spite of these instances of compassionate behavior, Douglass exhibited no
evidence of identification with them. Not only did he emotionally detach
himself from them when his mistress ceased to educate him and his
master let brandy influence his treatment, but he also refused to work
when Auld declined permission for his continuing to hire out his own
time. What is more, he determined to retaliate if Auld tried to whip him

for his refusal. Finally, he decided to escape from this "kind" slaveholding pair.

Douglass' first effort to escape was from another "kind" slavemaster, Mr. Freeland. Freeland "seemed to possess some regard for humanity."[33] An "open and frank master,"[34] he provided enough to eat as well as enough mealtime, worked his slaves but limited the hours, supplied proper tools, and employed enough assistance. Douglass considered Freeland "the best master I ever had," [35] but he wanted to be his own master. And so, it was from this "best master" that Douglass undertook his first flight from slavery. Neither in this instance nor in those of the "kind" Masters Anthony and Auld did Douglass demonstrate any inclination to identify with them. He considered all slaveholders bad, and did not want to live with even the "kindest" of them. He would have probably accredited much of that attitude to the "power of truth" unwittingly furnished by Auld.

Douglass' affection for other "kind" whites did not approach identification either. His first attachment came after Mrs. Sophia Auld abandoned his reading lessons. Determined to continue them, he made "friends of all the little white boys whom I met in the streets (and) converted (them) into teachers."[36] His strategy was to carry bread with him on his errands and barter the bread for his bread of life — education. When he prepared to leave the Hugh Auld family to live with Thomas Auld, he explained that the bond between the boys and him was stronger than his ties to the Auld family. One measure of his gratitude was his declining to reveal their names in the *Narrative* for fear of their being harassed. Douglass "loved" Mr. Cookman for the same reasons as did the other slaves of Thomas Auld; he discerned Cookman's sympathy for him. Douglass also held a high opinion of a Mr. Wilson, whom he met there, for Wilson "proposed to keep a Sabbath school for the instruction of such slaves as might be disposed to learn to read the New Testament."[37] Though ordered to stop after three lessons, he was never forgotten by Douglass. Douglass' fondness for those other "kind" whites was not identification; quite the contrary, he regarded each as a potential instrument of freedom.

Douglass' physical resistance to white oppression completed the psychological liberation that the "power of truth" of demystifying that oppression began. Even though he had been appalled by the different types of slave mistreatments, it was not until he secured this "power of truth" that he exhibited anger and hatred. Thus, the origin of his psychological liberation was also the genesis of his physical resistance. In fact, it became necessary for Douglass to physically resist oppression to claim and preserve his identity. Perhaps Frantz Fanon, Algerian revolutionary from Martinique, provides the cerebral link in *The Wretched of the Earth*:

> At the level of individuals, violence is a cleansing force. It frees the native from
> his inferiority complex and from his despair and inaction; it makes him fearless
> and restores his self-respect.[38]

Mr. Covey, the slavebreaker to whom Thomas Auld had sent him, became the object of Douglass' resistance. It could have been any man who symbolized enslavement. In this instance, three factors seemed to have combined to create Douglass' resolve to fight. First, there was the psychological support that the discovery of his identity yielded through the "power of truth" and the concomitant psychological resistance to encroachment on that identity. Second, there was the additional psychological support furnished by the root that Sandy Jenkins, an elderly slave, had advised him to wear on his right side to render himself immune to being whipped by a white man. Though Douglass doubted the efficacy of such a strategy, he reconsidered it when Covey, who had been waiting for Douglass to return to his farm so he could whip him, presented a kind demeanor upon first seeing him again. Although it was Sunday and it was possible that this was just Sunday behavior of the avowed Christian, Douglass "was half inclined to think the root to be something more than I at first had taken it to be."[39] Perhaps Covey was no more omnipotent than he was omnipresent — a prior apprehension of Douglass. Third, there was the immediate psychological support that Douglass garnered when Covey, "taken all aback...trembled like a leaf"[40] at Douglass' unexpected resistance to his whipping the following day. This assurance, conjoined with the first two factors, undercut Douglass' earlier fear, which had been partially responsible for his not taking Covey's life. Douglass describes the significance of self-defense on his identity:

> This battle with Covey was the turning point in my career as a slave. It rekin-
> dled the few expiring embers of freedom, and revived within me a sense of my
> own manhood. It recalled the departed self-confidence, and inspired me again
> with a determination to be free...He only can understand the deep satisfaction

which I experienced, who had himself repelled by force the bloody arm of slavery.
I felt as I never felt before. It was a glorious resurrection, from the tomb of slavery,
to the heaven of freedom. My long-crushed spirit rose, cowardice departed, bold
defiance took its place; and I now resolved that, however long I might remain a
slave in form, the day had passed forever when I could be a slave in fact.[41]

Douglass persisted in his determination never to be whipped again by
a white. Declaring "that the white man who expected to succeed in whipping, must also succeed in killing me,"[42] he was never again whipped
during his four remaining years as a slave. He indicated, however, that he
had several fights, one of which was with four white apprentice caulkers.
Even though his odds of winning the fight were negligible, he continued
to defend himself until fifty white ship-carpenters threatened to join the
caulkers. Sometime later, when Hugh Auld warned Douglass that he
would whip him for not hiring his time out one week to fatten Auld's
pockets, Douglass "resolved if he laid the weight of his hand upon me, it
should be blow for blow."[43] At sixteen, in his battle with Covey,
Douglass won his manhood; he never deigned to surrender it.

Douglass' identification with slaves was evident in three ways: 1) his
empathy with the effects of their not possessing the "power of truth" amid
"irresponsible power;" 2) his empathy with their miserable conditions;
and 3) his love for them, which was so often reflected in his actions.

Douglass believed that the "power of truth" gained by reading — the
potential power of such testimony to corroborate the witness of one's own
life — would cut through the slaveowners' psychological machinations,
breaking important links of their "irresponsible power." With that
freedom in mind, the slaves then needed to project corporal freedom
and/or be able to sustain an alternative community with its own identity
and values. Douglass thought that it would be more difficult for slaves to
negotiate the deceit that inhered in slavery without access to the language
of the deceivers. He suggested that the partial identification of slaves
with their owners was due to not being able to read the rules of the game.
He emphasized how his acquisition of the "power of truth" made it impossible to identify with even the "kindest" slaveowner.

Douglass also stressed the need for slaves to see the remedy to their
wretched condition in order not to despair and thus perpetuate "irresponsible power." His account of the songs of the slaves on their way to the
Great House Farm and the sadness of those songs intimated that the

privilege of the fleeting trip was the extent of this world's freedom. Whether the remedy was escape or a community based on common conditions, he alleged that the "power of truth" had to be connected to the power of hope to keep freedom on their minds. He was his own best example when he recounted how Covey made a slave from a man by crowding out the desire to confront slavery intellectually with the earthy fact of perpetual sweat. His spirit could not breathe in the suffocating air of such stringent physical demands, and despair attended even the stupor of the Sunday respite.

Douglass also identified with the atrocities visited upon slaves. First, he knew many of them firsthand. He was among those victims who did not precisely know his/her age; who had a white father; who was separated from his/her mother; who followed the condition of his/her mother; who knew hunger and cold; who experienced "can't see to can't see" travail, with the accompanying pain of the lash; and who remembered the abysmal indignities and anxieties of a property valuation.

Second, Douglass identified with many horrors to which he was not subjected. Even though the slave trade had long antedated Douglass' encounter with servitude, he related to the unspeakable horrors that the Africans endured. Although he probably was fathered by his first master, he apparently was not harassed by that master's mistress; yet he was moved by the plight of others. Douglass never was "convicted of any high misdemeanor, became unmanageable, or evinced a determination to run away"[44] — although he did make one unsuccessful attempt — but he knew slaves who were whipped and sold for any of these "irregularities." Even before he became a field hand, having known "kindness" in slaveowners, Douglass identified with other slaves at the property valuation of Captain Anthony who "were in very deed men and women of sorrow, and acquainted with grief...(and whose) backs had been made familiar with the bloody lash, so that they had become callous."[45] He was repulsed by the slavebreeding of Covey, and though it was outside the pale of his experience, he pitied especially the female victim.

Finally, though Douglass' second attempt to escape succeeded and he was not recaptured, he was yet sensitive to the "panting fugitive"[46] and his/her "danger of falling into the hands of money-loving kidnappers."[47] To reduce this danger, he chose "not to state all the facts connected with the transaction"[48] of his escape. Decrying such publicity by others, labelling it the "upperground railroad,"[49] he wanted instead the slaveholder attempting to return the fugitive to slavery "to imagine himself surrounded by myriads of invisible tormentors,"[50] and to imagine that he was "running the frightful risk of having his hot brains dashed out by an invisible agency."[51] Whether or not he had suffered the horrid condition, Douglass identified with slaves and, in the case of fugitive slaves, he courted the idea of violence to sustain their freedom.

Douglass' most convincing identification with slaves, however, was his activities in their behalf and the bedrock concern that undergirded them. While he was still yoked, he taught other slaves to read, and devised a strategy for those who wanted freedom as badly as he to accompany him in escaping. After he broke the chains of bondage, he began to subscribe to William Lloyd Garrison's paper, "Liberator," started to attend and speak at anti-slavery meetings, and, finally, wrote the *Narrative*. Douglass put his head and hands where his heart was.

Douglass' first contribution to the slaves was his teaching them how to read. While working for Mr. Freeland, he began by developing an interest to read in Freeland's two slaves. This interest soon spread to Freeland's hired hands and slaves on neighboring farms, and Douglass launched a "Sabbath school at the house of a free colored man, ...(having) at one time over forty scholars...of all ages, though mostly men and women."[52] The strength of Douglass' identification with them is revealed in his reflection upon the import of the Sabbath school in his life:

> I look back to those Sundays with an amount of pleasure not be expressed. They were great days to my soul. The work of instructing my dear fellow-slaves was the sweetest engagement with which I was ever blessed. We loved each other, and to leave them at the close of the Sabbath was a severe cross indeed.....I taught them, because it was the delight of my soul to be doing something that looked like bettering the condition of my race.[53]

In addition to the Sabbath school, Douglass later "devoted three evenings in the week, during the winter, to teaching the slaves at home."[54] He was gratified that several slaves learned to read and that at least one was free through his means.

Douglass also proffered the gift of freedom to the slaves. Resolving to make his bid for freedom during 1835, he desired their liberty as well, and so "commenced early...to imbue their minds with thoughts of freedom...(and) to impress them with the gross fraud and inhumanity of slavery."[55] Remembering the psychological boost that he had received from resisting oppression, Douglass argued that they could not keep claim to their manhood if they did not make at least one attempt to be free. Although their plan for escape was betrayed and they were apprehended, the intensity of their identification with each other is reflected in the fact that their primary concern, when examined for the passes that Douglass had written for them, was not to be separated. They considered this more important than the danger of being sold for their transgression against the "peculiar institution." Later, when the other slaves were taken from the jail, Douglass expresses that identification: "I regarded this separation as a final one. It caused me more pain than anything else in the whole transaction. I was ready for anything rather than separation."[56]

Perhaps even more revealing of Douglass' identification with the other slaves during his servitude at Freeland's was his feeling that the relative ease of his first year there owed in part to the communalism that the slaves developed:

> We were linked and interlinked with each other. I loved them with a love stronger than any thing I have experienced since. It is sometimes said that we slaves do not love and confide in each other....I never loved any or confided in any people more than my fellow-slaves, and especially those with whom I lived at Mr. Freeland's. I believe we would have died for each other....We never moved separately. We were one.[57]

A strong testimony, indeed. Later, when Douglass finally made his break from Hugh Auld to freedom, he emphasized that the largest pain in doing so was leaving the friends that he had established in Baltimore while hiring out his time. Although Douglass did not say — and some of those attachments may have been with whites, who, like the boy teachers, assisted him in his long journey to freedom — we may surmise that African-Americans, slave and/or free, were among those allegiances.

After Douglass reached free land, he continued to identify with slaves not only by almost questioning the righteousness of God in allowing the forced forfeiture of their bodies but also by working toward their freedom in three manners. First, after months in New Bedford, he subscribed to the "Liberator," a paper dedicated to the emancipation of slaves. Douglass' reaction to its good news is noteworthy:

Its sympathy for my brethren in bonds — its scathing denunciations of slave-holders — its faithful exposures of slavery — and its powerful attacks upon the upholders of the institution — sent a thrill of joy through my soul such as I had never felt before![58]

From the "Liberator," Douglass "got a pretty correct idea of the principles, measures and spirit of the anti-slavery reform,"[59] and it inspired his participation in the abolitionist struggle, his second service to the slaves. Though initially reluctant to voice his sentiments because he did not regard himself the equal of other speakers, he finally made the plunge at Nantucket, urged by a white abolitionist, William C. Coffin, as well as promoted by the increasing power of his own feelings. Douglass took the last step to his freedom as he put behind him the incompatible notions of being free and being a slave, of being equal and being unqualified to speak to whites. Douglass describes the historical beginning of his abolitionist career: "I spoke but a few moments, when I felt a degree of freedom, and said what I desired with considerable ease. From that time until now, I have been engaged in pleading the cause of my brethren."[60]

Douglass' third service to the slaves was the *Narrative*. Relying in part upon the "power of truth," the same power he identified while still a boy enraptured by *The Columbian Orator*, he hoped "that this little book may do something toward throwing light on the American slave system, and hastening the glad day of deliverance to the millions of my brethren in bonds."[61] With that faith in the power of the autobiography's demystification, Douglass pledged himself "anew to the sacred cause." [62]

Douglass' freedom brought him into increasing contact with other free African-Americans, and though his identification with them had already been grounded in his desire to be among their ranks and in the concrete association with the man at whose home he administered the Sabbath school, his new life reinforced that identification. Introduced to and assisted by the prominent abolitionists, Mr. David Ruggles and Rev. J.W.C. Pennington, in his enterprise for freedom, Douglass discovered two facts about free African-Americans that strengthened his identification. First, he learned that the material conditions of many of them surpassed those of the average slaveholders whom he had known in Maryland. In fact, he adjudged the material and cultural life of Mr. Nathan Johnson, who had suggested "Douglass" for his last name, to be superior to most of the slaveholders in Talbot County, Maryland. Second, he found a level of consciousness in free African-Americans that he had not anticipated: "I found the colored people much more spirited than I had supposed they would be. I found among them a determination to protect each other from a bloodthirsty kidnapper, at all hazards."[63]

Douglass' *Narrative* is a study of the "power of truth" triumphing over "irresponsible power." As the first major slave narrative, it is also the archetypal literary study of the myths of black identity and black ethos. We witness how Douglass thought that the "power of truth" was necessary to the slaves in order to demystify their predicament and to resist the dehumanization of an alien identity and ethos. We also see how important Douglass felt that power was to the discovery and maintenance of his own identity and communal values. How else, Douglass might add, could the son of a white man not introduced to African-American field labor until the age of sixteen yet follow his mother's condition into slavery and turn it back upon a father whose power was so irresponsible that he would not claim Douglass?

Dunbar's "Entire Truthfulness": "Stric'ly True"

So far as I could remember, Paul Dunbar was the only man of pure African blood
and of American civilization to feel the negro life esthetically and express it lyri-
cally. It seemed to me that this had come to its modern consciousness in him, and
that his brilliant and unique achievement was to have represented him as he found
him to be, with humor, with sympathy, and yet with what the reader must instinctively feel to be entire truthfulness.[1]

These words slid from the pen of William Dean Howells, the most in-
fluential literary critic of the late nineteenth century in this country; they
became part of one of the most famous introductions ever accorded a
book of African-American poetry by a white reviewer. The book was
Lyrics of Lowly Life, (1896) by Paul Laurence Dunbar, the first African-
American poet to achieve a national reputation and to attempt to earn a
living solely by writing. A proponent of realism, Howells lauded what he
termed the objectivity and truthfulness of Dunbar; a reflector of the
racism which kept the misappelation "negro" in the lower case, he continued by parroting the current idea of African-American limitations, and
averring "that it was this humorous quality which Mr. Dunbar has added
to our literature, and it would be this which would most distinguish him,
now and hereafter."[2] Dunbar later claimed that as useful as this preface
had been in putting his name on the tongues of the literati and selling
books, it was the hazard of his new fortune that it emphasized his dialect
pieces to the detriment of the standard English poems. Nor was it that he
repudiated his dialect work; rather, he desired equal time for both. This
author posits that the truthful glimpses into slave life added more to our
literature than the humor which Howells could not well refuse to enjoy.

The realities of slave life were not usually the more smiling aspects of American life and several of Dunbar's poems spoke to the sordid aspects of oppression. In this chapter, the author intends to show that some of Dunbar's dialect work — the standard English pieces are not considered here — was in fact strictly true in addressing the cultural repression of slaves. For our purposes we shall not examine dialect verse which evinces nostalgia for slavery if there is no attendant identification with the slavemaster. In fact, the author only locates three poems in Dunbar's published dialect work which reflect patent identification. (Perhaps, there was a method in Dunbar's reputed madness, after all.) Although these few poems will be explored for their commentary on slave mystification, we shall focus on his depiction of the oppression of slaves, their response to that oppression, and their racial pride. In these poems, Dunbar's slaves demystified the "peculiar institution" and illustrated the retention of black identity and a communal ethos. The author has chosen twenty-five narrative poems from Dunbar's six books of poetry to demonstrate this. First, however, for contextual reasons, the validity of his general image should be briefly examined, along with his own view of the dialect efforts.

Despite the recent efforts by a few critics like Houston A. Baker Jr. [3], Dickson D. Bruce[4], James A. Emmanuel[5], Gossie H. Hudson[6], and Darwin T. Turner[7] to reconstruct the image of Dunbar, he remains, in the opinion of most dilettantes of African-American literature, a lyrical Sambo who reinforced the grinning black caricatures of the Southern Plantation school of white writers such as Thomas Nelson Page, Joel Chandler Harris and Irwin Russell. Consequently, Dunbar embarrasses or repulses most young African-American readers. Judging him a casualty of W.E.B. DuBois' double consciousness, in that he rejected his blackness in favor of the song of the American siren, they smugly write him off as a black Judas, refusing to pay him a sliver of serious consideration.

Was he a traitor? Did he exhibit the tendency at best dormant in the most embittered African-Americans of paying obeisance to the dominant values of this society? He did manifest this urge, but he was not a traitor. I shall not attempt to vindicate the American side of his cultural duality; too much that he wrote did place the stamp of authenticity on the idea of the antebellum contented slave. But the verdict of turncoat even on the basis of these myth-reinforcing poems seems unfair because it does not fit him squarely in the context of his time — the time of Booker T. Washington accommodation, the time of blatant denials of the rights of black people, the time of their unspeakable physical abuse, even the time of sentimental James Whitcomb Rileyish poetry that fled the realities of late nineteenth century-industrial age horrors of robber baronism. Further, this judgment does not reflect Dunbar's personal aesthetic dilemma about the proper domain of poetry.

As Jay Martin explained, Dunbar held a "commitment to two sets of standards and values — in one group, to the aesthetic values residing in works of art; and in the other to the racial values residing in his community."[8] This quandary is reflected in two poems in which he expressed his aesthetic. "A Choice" reveals an art for art's sake orientation:

> They please me not — these solemn songs
> That hint of sermons covered up.
> 'Tis true the world should heed its wrongs,
>   But in a poem let me sup,
> Not simples brewed to cure or ease
> Humanity's confessed disease,
> But the spirit-wine of a singing line,
>   Or a dew-drop in a honey cup![9]

This view that poetry should not soil its hands with injustice was not uncommon, but for people who had been re-enslaved, "the spirit-wine of a singing line, or a dew-drop in a honey cup" did not drop the oppression from their lives. Yet Dunbar's plaudits in "James Whitcomb Riley" were the antithesis of that creed:

> Fur trim an' skillful phrases,
>   I do not keer a jot;
> 'Tain't the words alone, but feelin's,
>   That tech the tender spot.
>
> ....
>
> He paints our joys an' sorrers
>   In a way so stric'ly true,
> That a body can't help knowin'
>   That he has felt them too.
>
> ....

49

Now in our time, when poets rhyme
  For money, fun, or fashion,
'Tis good to hear one voice so clear
  That thrills with honest passion.[10]

Here, Dunbar would be accused of didactic poetry. But the "honest passion," and the "stric'ly true" version of sorrow are precisely what he wished to avoid, according to the philosophy of the first poem.

Finally, the ruling of traitor is unfair because it does not consider his temperament and his early life experiences. An early black biographer, Benjamin Brawley, who knew Dunbar's wife, Alice, well, believed him to be a man who by nature "was gentle, with a keen sense of the comedy in life."[11] Furthermore, most of Dunbar's critical associations were with whites. Not only was he the sole African-American in his high school class, but the most significant opportunities he received in his short poetic career came from whites. So, both his personal disposition and the positive nature of his contact with whites must be weighed in the balance.

Let us hear the conclusion of this matter. Dunbar was not a traitor; he was an African-American man in white America, and therein lay most of his contradictions. If he had not been black, the nineties would have been gay times, and his associations with and assistance from whites would have reinforced his identity and not assaulted it. Even the aesthetic dilemma would not have been as difficult to settle; he would not have been charged with parochialism, for his kind would have been universal. And thus, inherently, his poetry would have been art. Yes, Dunbar possessed amazing color in such circumstances.

As the author has suggested, the most resistant aspect of Dunbar's old image has been the negative implication of his dialect poems. Again, he did not reject those poems. In fact, on at least two occasions, he demonstrated a fondness for them as well as a sadness that they were often misapprehended. In an introduction to his poetry in *The Paul Laurence Dunbar Reader*, editors Jay Martin and Gossie Hudson revealed that "he told an English interviewer in 1897, I must confess my fondest love is for the Negro pieces...These little songs I sing because I must. They have grown instinctively in me."[12] In an earlier article in *Phylon*, Hudson cited Dunbar's response to Helen Douglass, the white wife of Frederick Douglass, who felt that some of his dialect work was debasing as minstrelsy: "As to your remarks about my dialect, I have nothing to say save that I am sorry to find among intelligent people those who are unable to differentiate dialect as a philosophical branch from Negro minstrelsy."[13]

Now that we have tested the fairness of Dunbar's treasonous image and the credence of the theory that he disesteemed his dialect poetry, let us briefly explore the three poems which evince slave mystification and then concentrate on the twenty-five which reflect a sense of the slaves' oppression, their reaction to that oppression, and an impression of racial pride, and thus see how Dunbar's slaves demystify the "peculiar institution" and resist the cultural repression of the colonizer.

The three poems of Dunbar which show poetic individuations of mystification are "The Deserted Plantation," "The News," and "Chrismus On The Plantation." In the first poem, an anonymous slave bemoans slave desertion of "de ole plantation." Remembering the glory of "de deah ole place," he finds in that recollection "all dat loved me an dat I love in de pas." Dunbar's slave is not just sentimentalizing about the joys of the erstwhile slave community; everyone is gone but him. Rather, he chooses to remain and serve the slavemaster " 'Twell de othah Mastah thinks it's time to end it,/An calls me to my qua'ters in de sky."[14]

The other two poems illustrate even more graphically slave identification with the colonizer. In "The News," an old slave is informed by his master's offspring that the plantation owner has been killed in the Civil War, and is ravaged. Lamenting that his infirmities prevented him from accompanying his master into battle, he asks to be placed near his owner's bed and wills his death in order to rejoin the colonizer:

Yes, suh, I's comin' ez fas'ez I kin,—
'T was kin' o' da'k, but hit's lightah agin:
P'omised yo' pappy I'd allus tek keer
Of you, — yes, mastah, — I's follerin', — hyeah![15]

Ol' Ben is the mystified slave of "Chrismus On The Plantation," although he seems to speak for the group who is notified on Christmas Eve before Emancipation by the slaveowner that the plantation must be sold. Ol' Ben emerges from the crowd and tells the colonizer that they should not be asked to forget his kindness and assures him that they will not abandon him in his helplessness: "Well, ef dat's de way dis freedom ac's on people, white er black,/ You kin jes' tell Mistah Lincum fu' to tek his freedom back."[16]

These three poems of Dunbar obviously display poetic individuations of mystification. But most of his dialect work — even the sentimental pieces — does not unmistakably reflect slave identification with the slavemaster. In fact, much of the dialect verse can be read as evidence of slave demystification. Let us now examine those twenty-five poems which are informed by slave awareness of their oppression and a sense of self.

Ten poems reflect the actualities of black oppression. In "A Banjo Son," the "weary slave" testifies that "de pleasures of dis life is few enough."[17] "Parted," though some believe that it de-emphasizes the cruelties of slave existence, reflects the knowledge of the male that families were arbitrarily broken for profits, and that the "ship" and "chain" were soon to confront him.[18] "When Sam'l Sings" mirrors this same phenomenon, but the "trouble" and "strife" fade as Sam contemplates seeing his wife.[19] The narrator in "Long To'ds Night" realizes that "wo'kin putty nigh done made/him dumb."[20] The slave in "A Plantation Melody" expresses his view of life:

O brothah, w'en de tempes' beat,
An' w'en yo' weary head an' feet
   Can't fin' no place to res'
....

O sistah, w'en de rain come down,
An' all yo' hopes is 'bout to drown,
   Don't trus de Mastah less.[21]

"Dreamin' Town" suggests the problems of slave life by implication and symbolism. The speaker asks Mandy Lou, "Ain't you tiahed of every day," and urges her to "Come away to dreamin' town," promising her the following conditions:

Whaih de skies don't nevah frown
....
Whaih de streets is paved with gol',
Whaih de days is nevah col',

An' no sheep strays f'om de fol'

....

Whaih our hands an' he'ats are free

....

Whaih de fruit is bendin' down.[22]

Only in protecting free hands and hearts does the poet not employ symbolism in his implying slavery's severity. The frowning skies probably represent a general condition of hardship; the golden streets may suggest that slavery is a rough road as well as a poverty-stricken one; the cold days no doubt refer to the temperament of the masters or the overall coldness of the slave situation; the sheep perhaps are the runaways who stray perforce; and the fruit is obviously food or the material life in general. In "Little Brown Baby," the father realizes the tyranny that the child will soon confront and tells him that he "Wisht you could allus know ease an' cleah skies;/Wisht you could stay jes' a chile on my breas'—."[23] In W'en I Gits Home," the slave, who has "sorrer," "woe," and "caihs," sees the country as "dis grieving' lan'" where "de road is rough."[24] "Speakin' In De Cou'thouse" reveals in the last two lines that for every politician who opposed the slave cause there was a "jones nex' week" who supported it.[25] "The Old Cabin" registers the feeling of a slave, who although he recalls the pleasant memories of his African-American friends and children, also remembers "de days w'en slavery helt me/In my misery — ha'd an' fas;" remembers a "mighty tryin" time, "de whuppins" and "de feah o' block an' lash."[26]

These ten poems, then, project slaves who would not have considered slavery a blessing, because they had demystified their servitude. They found their bondage tempestuous, with few enchantments. As they considered the broken families, the whippings, the auction block, and the duplicity of politicians, they deemed America a place of sorrow from which they desired to release their children.

Fifteen of the poems, including some with references to oppression, contain allusions to the slave response to that oppression. Six of them mention the joy felt in contemplating or experiencing time that was their own. "Chrismus On The Plantation," a poem cited earlier which has rightfully elicited severe criticism for its notion of the devoted ex-slaves whose loyalty to their former master outstrips their own desire for freedom, explains nonetheless that "a da'ky's allus happy when de holidays is neah."[27] "Back-Log Song" also characterizes this sentiment at Christmas:

> An' ouah hea'ts are full of pleasure, fu' we know de time is ouahs
> Fu' to dance er do jes' whut we wants to do.
> An' dey ain't no ovahseer an' no othah kind o' powahs
> Dat kin stop us while dat log is bu'nin' thoo.[28]

Anticipating the temporary relief, the slave in "Chrismus Is A-Coming" declares that "Chrismus day's a-comin/and all de week is ouahs."[29] The slave rejoices that "Missus gone a-drivin," Mastah gone to shoot, in "A Warm Day in Winter."[30] "Long To'ds Night" describes the reaction of the slave as he anticipates the end of the long day:

> Daih's moughty soothin' feelin'
> Hits a dahky man,
>   'Long to'ds night.

The slave "mence to sing," "keepin' time a-steppin'/Wid a little song,"/ "An de sweat roll down his forred,/Mixin' wid his smile,"/and "Dey's a moughty glory in him/Shinin' thoo his face,"/because "De wo'kin' all is ovah." He considers that "De wo'kin time's Decembah, but de restin' time is June," concluding "W'y, hit's blessid, jes' a- livin' w'en a body's wo'k is done/'Long to'ds night."[31] Finally, in "A Frolic," the slave dancers are reminded that "Mastah gone to town tonight;/'Tain't no time to walk." It's time to "bow an' p'omenade."[32]

Among the other poems depicting reactions to slavery, the most frequently quoted is no doubt "An Ante-Bellum Sermon," in which the sagacious slave preacher communicates a revolutionary message guised in biblical terms. To illustrate this typical situation in slave religion requires the citation of several passages. The poem opens:

> We is gathahed hyeah, my brothahs,
>   In dis howlin' wildaness,
> Fu' to speak some words of comfo't
>   To each othah in distress.
> An' we chooses fu' ouah subjic'
>   Dis — we'll 'splain it by an'by;

"An' de Lawd said, 'Moses, Moses,'
An' de man said, "Hyeah am I.'"[33]

After telling the biblical story of Moses and the hardhearted Pharaoh
who refused to let the Jewish slaves go, the minister applies the interven-
tion of God to their own bondage:

Fu' de Lawd will he'p his chillun,
    You kin trust him evah time.
....
But de Lawd will sen' some Moses
    Fu' to set his chillun free.[34]

However, given the possible presence of black informers, he hastens to
add:

But fu' feah some one mistakes me,
    I will pause right hyeah to say,
Dat I'm still a-preachin' ancient,
    I ain't talkin' 'bout to-day.
....
Now don't run an' tell ya' mastahs
    Dat I's preachin' discontent
....
'Cause I isn't; I'se a-judgin'
    Bible people by deir ac's;
I'se a-given' you de Scriptuah,
    I'se a-handin' you de fac's.[35]

After reminding them again of the power of God, he says that there are
contemporary Pharaohs who deny the Lord's intention that "His almighty
freedom/should belong to evah man."[36] Once again, he hurries to dismiss
any accusation that he is spreading dissatisfaction:

But I think it would be bettah,
    Ef I'd pause agin to say,
Dat I'm talkin' 'bout ouah free'dom
    In a Bibleistic way.[37]

The final stanza combines the idea of an African-American leader who will emancipate his people with a last-line prod that he is just preaching the gospel:

> But when Moses wif his powah
>   Comes an' sets us chillun free,
> We will praise de gracious Mastah
>   Dat has gin us liberty;
> An' we'll shout ouah halleluyahs,
>   On dat mighty reck'nin' day,
> When we'se reco'nised ez citiz'—
>   Huh uh! Chillun, let us pray![38]

The remaining poems of slave response are varied. "Accountability" reflects the common notion that a slave, who was property, could not, by definition, steal property. When the slave asks his wife to "go put on de kittle" to cook one of his master's chickens, he is subscribing to the situational ethics so customarily practiced by the slaves.[39] "A Banjo Song" documents the functionability of music in black lives — an African orientation — as it is used to restore the spirit:

> Oh, de music o' de banjo,
>   Quick an deb'lish, solemn, slow,
> Is de greates' joy an' solace
>   Dat a weary slave kin know![40]

"Parted," though often observed as a poem which suggests a too heavy reliance on God to make the situation bearable, reflects, in fact, the courage so characteristic of slaves and a God operative in this life Who would assist him in returning. The husband understands the cruelty of the system and voices his agony that "I knowed some day we'd have to pa't,/But den hit put' nigh breaks my hea't."[41] So, he consoles his wife, attempting to strengthen her spirit for the approaching disunion:

> Ole Mas' done sol' me down de stream;
> Dey tell me 'tain't so bad's hit seem,
> ....

I'll stan' de ship, I'll stan' de chain.[42]

When he asserts that "God know ouah hea'ts, my little dove/; He'll he'p us f'om his th'one above,"[43] one could make a case that in the line, "But den I do' know what to do,"[44] he is considering escape, and that he is so confident of God's assistance, he says "D' ain't nothin' dat kin keep me 'way."[45]

Another poem, "When Sam'l Sings," also particularizes the strength of slave marriages. Both Sam'l and the narrator find reservoirs of will in their relationships. The narrator limns Sam'l's situation:

> Sam'l smilin' an' a-singin'
>   'Case he been to see his wife.
> ....
> She live on de fu' plantation,
>   Twenty miles erway er so;
> But huh man is mighty happy
>   W'en he git de chanst to go.
> ....
> Walkin' allus ain' de nices'—
>   Mo'nin fin's him on de way—
> But he allus comes back smilin',
>   Lak his pleasure was his pay.
> ....
> "Whut's de use o' havin' trouble,
>   What's de use o' havin' strife?"
> Dat's de way dis Sam'l preaches
>   W'en he been to see his wife.[46]

"A Christmas Folksong" might be read as an authentication of strong family ties. The speaker, visualizing the church cemetery, pours out his grief:

> Dey's Allen on de hillside,
>   An Marfy in de plain;
> ....
> Dey's Ca'line, John, an' Susie
>   Wid only dis one lef':[47]

Two poems deal with the familiar response of slaves when provided a chance to help effect their own freedom in the Civil War. "Whistling Sam" indicates the pride that they felt:

At de call fu' colo'ed soldiers, Sam enlisted 'mong de res'
Wid de blue o' Gawd's great ahmy wropped about his swellin' breas',
An' he laffed an' whistled loudah in his youfful joy an' glee
Dat de govament would let him he'p to mek his people free.[48]

In "When Dey "Listed Colored Soldiers," the same sense of importance is delineated. The speaker explains the reply of her man, 'Lias, to her request not to go:

But he tol' me dat his conscience, hit was callin' to him so,
An' he couldn't baih to lingah w'en he had a chanst to fight
For de freedom dey had gin him an' de glory of de right.[49]

She then informs us of how her grief turns to pride:

W'y my hea't nigh broke wid grievin' twell I seed him on de street;
Den I felt lak I could go an' th'ow my body at his feet.
For his buttons was a-shinin', an' his face was shinin', too,
An' he looked so strong an' mighty in his coat o' sojer blue,
Dat I hollahed, "Step up, manny."[50]

The poem also gives insight into the verities of slave grief resulting from the war. In two different places, we are told that she did not identify with the misery of injury or death in the South, now that her 'Lias was fighting in the Union army:

Bofe my mastahs went in gray suits, an' I loved de Yankee blue,
But I t'ought dat I could sorrer for de losin' of 'em too;
But I couldn't, for I didn't know de ha'f o' whut I saw,
"Twell dey 'listed colo'ed sojers an' my 'Lias went to wah.
....
W'en de women cried an' mou'ned 'em, I could feel it thoo an' thoo,
For I had a loved un fightin' in de way o' dangah, too.[51]

She relates to their sorrow, but only through her feeling for 'Lias. When she is apprised of his death, she is distressed, but it does not annihilate her pride:

> Den dey tol' me dey had laid him some'r's way down souf to res'
> Wid de flag dat he had fit for shinin' daih acrost his breas'.
> Well, I cried, but den I reckon dat's what Gawd had called him for,
> W'en dey 'listed colo'ed sojers an' my 'Lias went to wah.[52]

The last three poems suggest slave grief, but one unmixed with pride. "W'en I Gits Home" reflects the slave's reactions of weariness and sorrow. He is "tiahed of dis grievin' lan...an' wid woe."[53] In "A Plantation Melody," the narrator gives the lie to the happy, contented slave myth:

> I's 'lone an' in distress.
> ....
> My po' sick hea't is trimblin' so,
>   It hu'ts my very breas'.[54]

"Philosophy" typifies the response of slaves when oppression was so weighty that they could not even force the corners of the mouths up in pretense. It is a rejoinder to a white preacher who had counseled them to wear continuous smiles:

> But you don't ketch folk a-grinnin'wid a misery in de back;
> An' you don't fin dem a-smilin' w'en dey's hongry ez kin be,
> Leastways, dat's how human natur' allus seems to 'pear to me.
> ....
> We is mos' all putty likely fu' to have our little cares,
>   An' I think we'se doin' fus' rate w'en we jes' go long and bears,
> Widout breakin' up ouah faces in a sickly so't o grin,
>   W'en we knows dat in ouah innards we is p'intly mad ez sin.
> ....
> Oh dey's times fu' bein' pleasant an' fu' goin' smilin' roun',
>   'Cause I don't believe in people allus totin' roun' a frown,
> But it's easy 'nough to titter w'en de stew is smokin' hot,
>   But hit's mighty ha'd to giggle w'en dey's nuffin' in de pot.[55]

These fifteen poems suggest slaves who were happy and content only when they owned their time; were taking back compensation that had been stolen from them; were together with their spouses, other members of the family, or members of their religious family; were planning their escapes; or were afforded a chance to fight for their freedom. Generally weary and sad, they found some solace in music or in the expectation of concrete divine assistance. Often, they did not grin but just bore it. Dunbar's slaves demystified their servitude, and although they recognized the possibility of traitors among them, keeping their minds on freedom, they resisted their dehumanization by appropriating their own space with those they loved.

Finally, ten poems assault the historical exaggeration of self-hatred in slavery. All evince racial pride. Four of them contradict that part of the overstatement which claims that slaves loathed the color of their skin and the tight circles of their hair. In "Little Brown Baby," it is "Little brown baby wif spa'klin eyes," who is daddy's "darlin'," "chile," "pa'dner," "playmate," and "joy."[56] "Dreamin' Town" also celebrates the skin of Blacks when the speaker exhorts Mandy Lou to "Smooth your brow of lovin' brown" when she arrives at his "dreamland town" which is free of slavery's problems.[57] In "A Plantation Portrait," both the skin and hair of African-Americans are extolled. Mandy Lou is

> Browner den de frush's wing,
> ....
> An' huh haih a woolly skein,/Black an' plain.
> Hol's you wid a natchul twis'/Close to bliss.[58]

Yet, surely the strongest example is "Dely." The following excerpts show how a Dunbar slave glorified the eyes, hair and skin of Blacks:

> Dely got dem meltin' eyes,
>   Big an' black an' tendah.
> ....
> Dely brown ez brown kin be
>   An' huh haih is curly;
> Oh, she look so sweet to me,—
> ....

Dely brown ez brown kin be,
    She ain't no mullatter;
She pure cullud, — don' you see
    Dat's jes' whut's de mattah?
Dat's de why I love huh so,
    D'ain't no mix about huh,
Soon's you see huh face you know
    D'ain't no chanst to doubt huh.

      ....

I jes' sets an looks at huh,
    Dat's enuff 'uligion.[59]

This slave contradicts the myth that all slaves disassociated themselves from the African phenotype, reflecting a wish to be as white as possible.

Three other poems vaunt blackness by submitting that whites are inferior in certain respects. Both "When Malindy Sings" and "The Colored Band" declare what was commonly believed among slaves: that blacks possess more musical endowment than whites. In the first, the advice and analysis offered the white Miss Lucy is explicit:

G'way an' quit dat noise, Miss Lucy—
    Put dat music book away;
What's dat de use to keep on tryin'?
    Ef you practise twell you're gray,
You cain't sta't no notes a-flyin'
    Lak de ones dat rants and rings
F'om de kitchen to de big woods
    When Malindy sings.

      ....

You ain't got de nachel o'gans
    Fu' to make de soun' come right,
You ain't got de tu'ns an' twistin's
    Fu' to make it sweet an' light.[60]

The latter poem claims the superiority of the colored band, "Fu' de music dat dey mekin' can't be beat."[61] A comparison with a white band provides the reasons:

You kin hyeah a fine perfo'mance w'en de white ban's serenade,
    An' dey play dey high-toned music mighty sweet,
But hit's Sousa played in ragtime, an' hit's Rastus on Parade,
    W'en de colo'ed ban' comes ma'chin down de street.
....

Oh, de white ban' play hits music, an' hit's mighty good to hyeah,
An' it sometimes leaves a ticklin' in yo' feet;
But de hea't goes into bus'ness fu' to he'p erlong de eah,
    W'en de colo'ed ban' goes ma'chin down de street.[62]

The third poem, "Possum," asserts that whites don't know how to eat. The speaker is flustered by their style of cooking the possum:

Ef dey's anyt'ing dat riles me
....
Hit's to see some ign'ant white man
    'Mittin dat owdacious sin—
....
White folks t'ink dey know 'bout eatin',
    An' I reckon dat dey do
....
But dey ain't a t'ing dey knows of
    Dat I reckon cain't be beat
W'en we set down at de table
    To a unskun possum's meat![63]

The final poems exhibit a commonplace pride in the family and a sense of community. Slaves thought as much of their children as the masters did of theirs. The speaker destroys any contrary idea in "Chrismus Is A-Comin'":

Ol' Mas' Bob an' Missis
In dey house up daih
Got no chile lak dis is,
D'ain't non anywhaih.[64]

In "Long To'ds Night," the narrator's "wife look moughty lakly, an de chile de puttiest one."[65] "The Old Cabin" manifests a sense of community even in the midst of servitude. As the slave reminisces about the past, he admits his sorrow:

An hit hu'ts me w'en I membahs
  Dat I'll nevah see no mo'
Dem ah faces gethered smilin'
  Roun' dat po' ol' cabin do'.[66]

These ten poems depict slaves who were proud of their physical features, if not convinced that the more African traits were superior to the mix introduced by the masters. African-Americans were clearly superior in musical aptitude and the quality of the palate. Finally, not only did they not despise, but they loved their children, wives/husbands, and possessed a striking sense of community. Dunbar's slaves resisted the dehumanization of extrinsic identity and values, reinforcing the African idea that black and we are both beautiful.

These last twenty-five poems do not cancel out mawkish ones; that was not the aim of this perusal. In fact, this author has implied that they deserve another reading if excessive sentimentalism about slavery is not accompanied by slave identification with the slavemaster. In this survey, the poems of our focus do demonstrate an extent of racial consciousness in Dunbar's dialect work that heretofore has not been established. Critics often single out a poem or two that exhibit black awareness, intimating if not openly declaring that the rest of his attempts in black vernacular should be relegated to the junk heap of writings by schizoid African-American poets. But there is a pattern here. These slaves of Dunbar are not the ciphers of Ulrich Phillips or the "Sambos" of Stanley Elkins. They are real and it is this "entire truthfulness" of their subjugation, their consciousness of it, and the incredible openings that they wedged in the cultural repression of the colonizers toward the myths of black identity and black ethos that make these lyrics of Dunbar "stric'ly true."

V

Visible Nationalism
in *Invisible Man*

Ralph Waldo Ellison is not a nationalist. Repeatedly, over the thirty-seven years since the publication of his tour de force, *Invisible Man,* he has denied any sympathy for the black nationalist movement in this country. Denigrating political artists, he has argued for a non-sociological, universal writing. Despite the fact that the deepening of the particular experience is the surest route to universality, and that all art reflects some aspects of the evolution of a society — the forms, institutions and functions of its human groups — Ellison insists on such distinctions. To quarrel with him, however, is not the aim of this chapter. Rather, it is to show that one can perform a nationalistic reading of the brilliant novel by examining some of the characters. It will be demonstrated that at least seven personalities exhibit behavior that ranges from nascent black nationalism to revolutionary black nationalism, moving as such in the direction of the myths of black identity and black ethos. Further, we shall see that the sense of black nationalism in the characters assists them in demystifying their experiences with whites and African-American plenipotentiaries, (or in helping the Hero demystify his experiences) and that their organizational activities contribute to their resistance of dehumanization.

First, we need to define black nationalism. For our purposes here, let us emphasize two widely agreed upon elements: a feeling of racial solidarity, whether from positive or negative experiences, and a desire to organize around that solidarity. Although most of the nationalism in the novel reflects only the first factor, the second does exist. Because an understanding of the nationalism of six of the characters will shed light on any such tendencies in the Hero, let us examine them first and in the order of their appearance.

The grandfather, who appears only in the mind of the Hero, must yet be considered as a very real figure. He exerts a profound influence on the nameless one; in fact, his deathbed advice of undermining whites with smiles and agreeing finally becomes the source to which the Hero returns for his answer to a plan of action for his future emergence from underground. The grandfather had labeled himself a traitor and a spy in the enemy's country, a man who not only perceived all life for African-Americans as war, but who actually at one time believed in physical self-defense. The portrait suggested by this advice is strengthened by dream and memory references. In a dream which the Hero experiences as the night of the battle royal and Booker T. Washington's speech, the absent mentor not only refuses to laugh at the clowns in the circus but leads him to discovery of a "Keep This Nigger-Boy Running" note, which presages the Bledsoe letter. As the grandfather consistently intrudes into his thoughts, the Hero reminisces about that dissenting voice, his introduction of Frederick Douglass, the harsh terms he reserved for Uncle Toms, his counsel of not permitting whites to confide in you due to their potential subsequent shame and hate, and even the fact that the subversive "Swing Low, Sweet Chariot" was his favorite spiritual. At the end of the story, the Hero concludes, despite his grandfather's opinion that whites hate blacks, that he was a very humane person. In sum, the grandfather was a nationalist of the first type; perhaps, the innuendos regarding organization would suggest a place in the second rank as well. His views, advice, and dream presence aid the Hero in demystifying his experiences with whites and understanding their attempt to dehumanize him.

The vet, whom the Hero meets at the Golden Day, also harbors nationalist sentiments. Initially impressed by the fearless manner in which the vet approached Mr. Norton, a rich white philanthropist who is supporting the black college that the Hero attends, the invisible man is subsequently subjected to the vet's notions of his lack of blackness. Referring to the Hero as a zombie, a mechanical man because he accepts the paternalistic arrangements in the southern black school, the vet suggests that he is Fanon's black man with a white mask. Though ostensibly insane, the vet commands a sense of respect from the Hero. Later, after he is summarily dismissed from the college by Bledsoe, the fawning president, he encounters the vet on the bus that he is riding to New York. The vet, always using the pronoun "they" to refer to whites, encourages the Hero to exploit their blindness, to define the rules of the game. He admonishes him to be his own man, to never be servile before the Nortons of the world. The vet seems to possess a genuine sense of blackness, and espouses self-determination. Both these exhortations and his manner of relating to Mr. Norton establish him as a nationalist in our first sense. They also help the Hero demystify his encounters with whites and their sycophantic black accomplices.

Mary Rambo, the earth-mother type, demonstrating the extended family orientation of blacks by taking the Hero in her small home, also exhibits race consciousness in her exchanges with him. Always speaking in terms of the collective "we," she urges him to be responsible, a leader, a credit to his people. She believes in young African-Americans, especially ones from the South. She disparages those who abandon their people after finding a niche in the system. Even though the Hero cannot understand the inner security that would permit her to own a cast iron bank in the shape of a dark-skinned black man, he considers her a stabilizing force that links him to the past. The blues-singing, cabbage-cooking widow inspires hope in him, irrespective of the resentment he often feels toward her quiet pressure to succeed. "Miss Mary" wants African-Americans to retain their southern communal ways; in fact, she epitomizes them. On such basis, she would be classified as a nationalist of the racial-solidarity type. However, her faith that young Blacks as a group will lift all the race certainly implies organization, and possibly a berth for her in the second class. She is a constant reminder to the Hero that he must oppose the dehumanizing ethos of white individualism and lift his people as he climbs.

The Hero sees the image of his grandfather in Brother Tarp of the Brotherhood, finding him to be as much an admirer of Frederick Douglass as was his deceased ancestor. Offering the Hero a portrait of the nonpareil abolitionist to hang in his new office, Tarp suggests that it might hearten him in his new work as a Harlem agent for the Brotherhood, insisting that the nineteenth-century activist belonged to all black people. In addition, after relating the horrendous experience of some nineteen and a half years on the chain gang, Tarp hands him the link that he had cut in escaping. Although working in an interracial organization, Tarp proposes that the price of steel might remind the Hero of the real aims of their struggle. That Tarp saw the Brotherhood as a way to fight African-American oppression is confirmed by his ceasing to work for them when the organization stops its work in Harlem. Brother Tarp, a believer in racial solidarity, nevertheless assumes as have many black nationalists that the fight against racial oppression can best be waged in a Marxist structure. He is a force in keeping the Hero's mind on African-American freedom as well as a source of penetrating white Marxist paternalism and so demystifying their commitment to the black struggle.

Tod Clifton also initially proclaims Marxism. Introduced to the Hero in a strategy meeting to plan how to maximize the Harlem response to the eviction speech, he exerts a major influence on the development of the invisible man's nationalism. A disciple of Garvey, though at the time a Marxist, the nationalist strain wins out. The struggle, although enigmatic, is a predictable one. At the outset, the Hero detects an aloofness and questioning in Clifton's contact with the group. Later, Clifton broaches the subject of Garvey, marveling at the organizing success of the late Pan-Africanist, predicting an approximate triumph for the both of them. Though forced to defend himself in an attack at that meeting by Ras, the avowed black nationalist, Clifton is patently intrigued by this apparently new version of Garvey, his verbal denials notwithstanding. Unable to effectively challenge the rhetorical denunciations of their being Marxists, Clifton's frustration becomes anger, and he knocks Ras to the ground. Later, he juxtaposes two comments to the Hero which anticipate his subsequent actions. He observes that Ras is dangerous on the inside — the inside of Harlem as well as a black man's head — adding that sometimes one has to "plunge outside history," the ostensible scientific historical analysis of Marx. Clifton is also capable of violence against whites, ironically from the same frustration of seeking answers to African-American oppression that moved him to advance against Ras. When the Brotherhood finally reflects the interests of whites in their abandonment of work in Harlem, he withdraws, plunging outside history, attempting at once to use Brotherhood identification to punish them and avenging African-Americans by selling grotesque black paper dolls, showing them that their role in the organization is one of dancing Sambos. Clifton, always subscribing to racial solidarity whether as a Marxist or Garvey devotee, belongs to both orders of nationalists. He, even more than Brother Tarp, contributes to the Hero's demystification of white Marxist motives.

Ras the Exhorter — Ras the Destroyer — is the only avowed Pan-Africanist in the work. In his provocative exchange with the Hero and Clifton after his group attempts to physically oust the Brotherhood form

Harlem, he reveals the stuff of which nationalism is made. He issues several judgements of whites: 1) they hate blacks; 2) they were the enslavers and still exploit blacks for power and capital; 3) they use white women to bait black men into the movement; 4) their Marxist ideology is corrupt, and no white man's theory can solve black problems; 5) they offer blacks blood money to join their organizations; 6) they cause blacks to oppose each other; 7) they do not need to be allies with blacks, for they already have what they want; 8) their time of world domination is approaching an end; 9) they contaminate blacks with their amalgamative efforts; and 10) they persuade blacks not to trust their own intelligence. In his effort to proselyte the two black men, Ras pronounces certain determinations for blacks. Although some are implicit in the above condemnations of whites, others exist: 1) blacks should never collaborate with whites; 2) blacks should always be mindful of their African heritage; 3) since black blood built this country's civilization, only white blood can make recompense; 4) all blacks are brothers; 5) blacks in white movements betray their own people; 6) a black movement must be constructed; 7) Blacks who fight each other possess no self-respect; 8) blacks must keep whites out of Harlem; 9) black, brown, and yellow allies are sufficient; and 10) it is the duty of blacks to join a movement of their own. Although some of these pronouncements overlap, they incontestably demonstrate that Ras is a nationalist on both plateaus. Although the Hero is not privy to all of these views and does not have the personal contact that he has with Clifton, Ras makes a profound impact, helping him both to demystify his association with whites and to resist the dehumanization of being defined and exploited by them, even as Ras pursues his own egocentric objectives.

And now the Hero. Many articles have been written on the invisible man's search for his identity. Here, we shall only be concerned with that as it relates directly to a sense of racial solidarity and organizing on that basis. For clarity, the author will organize that evidence in eight sections: 1) pre-eviction speech, 2) eviction speech, 3) Harlem rally speech, 4) Tod Clifton association (including the funeral speech), 5) Ras conflict, 6) Harlem exchange, 7) Harlem riot, and 8) the underground ratiocination.

Prior to the eviction speech, the Hero's sense of racial solidarity is implicit. As early as his graduation day, he informs us that his grandfather's influence prevents him from believing the humility-equals-progress theme of his own oration. And in spite of the dream circuses at the battle royal and the state college for blacks, he has an impulse to spit on the blonde, to topple Mr. Colcord, and to share in the power of the vet and Dr. Bledsoe which enables them to verbally affront or manipulate the Mr. Nortons. He recognizes that blacks at the school have accepted white symbols, that many of the local whites were reared by black mammies, and that the gray-haired Miss Susie Greshams of black schools are not only warm matrons but also a link to slavery. After his expulsion from college, he is comfortable with Peter Wheatstraw and his jive language, and reconnects himself with the South and all that it means with the holy yam. And the virtually subdued anger of the past toward whites rises in his reactions to Kimbro, his white boss at Liberty Paints; in his lobotomy-aborted response to a racial insult at the hospital; and in his urge to smash the skin-whitening sign, which reminds him of who sets the standards in this society. And finally, he meets Mary Rambo, mirror image of the mothers he knew back home. He finds living with her pleasant, finds her a force riveting him to his roots, finds a source of hope for the future. Yes, the Hero often exhibits only an implicit nationalism in comparison with its subsequent explicitness, but these memories of home, school, and even the church reflect a veritable sense of racial solidarity. And in spite of the negative Booker T. Washington nationalism which characterizes his involvement in the imaginative battle royal and at the state college, he obviously sees whites as "they."

The event with the little old woman who lived in men's shoes intensifies this nationalism. The eviction scene evinces a Hero who not only is struck by the historical mementos of the elderly couple but also by his anger and the fear that his anger and his people's anger will result in justificatory violence. At this point, he is compelled to help avert the apocalypse. Though initially his call for organization is of the Booker T. Washington type, he is pulled by the pair to a higher level where he completely identifies with them. He reminds them of the commonality of their physical features, of the historical ties that they represent, of the failure of their dreams and its implications for them; and in a brilliant metaphor where whites become the law, he reminds them of their fulfillment. When the Brotherhood surfaces in white, he impulsively decries their claim of friendship to the ancient pair and infuriates Brother Jack by explaining his interest in the two in terms of race. What manner of man is this who now exclaims his people are dispossessed? Surely a nationalist in Harlem!

Neither Harlem nor the eviction removes the ambiguities of the invisible man, for he is no Ras, not even a Clifton. But in subsequent situations, we witness again the pull of the nationalist. The next major event seems to be the Harlem rally. Ironically, sporting an identity provided by whites, he is drawn back to himself by the southern-revival atmosphere which precedes his speech. He speaks to the black group in terms of "we," reviving their oppressive treatment, including the condescension that they met. He reminds them of their common dispossession, but also places some of the blame in their laps, suggesting that resistance is the only remedy. The truth of what he is saying, in addition to the truth of physical proximity to his people, raises him to a pitch of identifying Harlem as his home, his country, with its inhabitants not only his people but also the bearers of his vision. He also raises himself out of the sober, scientific theory of the Brotherhood — or we should say that he plunges outside history again in his second speech to blacks. Even after he is ordered to stay out of Harlem temporarily as a consequence of the Brotherhood's irritation at his emotionalism, he realizes that his words have been sincere in both instances, that the truth of them have possessed him.

The Hero's association with Tod Clifton bears enormous consequences. Clifton's attraction to Garvey, his fascination with Ras, as well as his compulsion to strike out physically at the Pan-Africanist in the absence of a rhetorical defense of belonging to a white-dominated Marxist organization, all puzzle the invisible man. Clifton's tears at the conclusion of his exchange with Ras, as well as his verbalized bewilderment at how black men preserve their sanity if they come to understand black history, further nonplus him. Not even the disappearance of Clifton from the Harlem district, abandonment of that area by the Brotherhood, their excluding the Hero from a crucial policy meeting, or finally Clifton's reappear- ance with the Sambo dolls serve much to ameliorate that confusion. Although the Hero never fully grasps the implications of his deceased associate's act of apparent self-mockery, he does begin to realize something of the meaning of Clifton's life. On the subway, he sees three black ghetto boys with magazines; and in the emotional, unscientific clutch of Clifton's death, he is seized by the thought that these men to be are outside history, and that it is his job to give them entry. In the Harlem streets, he notices the scores of blacks as though for the first time. He notices the resemblance between them and blacks down South; witnesses that the scientific Brotherhood has wrought no change in their lives; and understands that since the histories of peoples diverged long ago, one must begin with one's own history, one's own people if those histories are ever again to converge. His funeral address both reinforces and reflects this new awareness. Although unable to admit the unspeakable possibility that Clifton had considered him a sell-out, he now perceives that the Brotherhood, if not all whites, possesses the power to manipulate Blacks even as Clifton called the shots with an invisible black thread. But Clifton was a noble man, and he uses the funeral to restore that nobility. And that day, with the strains of "Many a Thousand Gone" bursting on his ears, he senses something far more profound than the theory of the Brotherhood. He sees that one must appropriate the imposed segregation of blacks with its attendant privity and power as a force toward ultimate and authentic integration. He reflects this yet recent discovery by informing the crowd that Clifton had thought the Brotherhood would make him more human, that working in an integrated group was already the way to halt black oppression. He also suggests that they organize to prevent another such senseless death. This sense of guilt of having belonged to the organization, of having been carried away by the notion of premature integration is the legacy of Clifton. And it is the concomitant responsibility that he carries underground to mull.

After futilely attempting to convince the Brotherhood of the reality of Harlem, and hearing Jack's claim to be their leader and therefore his, yet two more events strengthen the Hero's own conversion. The conversation with Brother Hambro is the first, and it follows his experience with posing as Rinehart, the Harlem chameleon, an experience that persuades him that the world is without boundaries and so it is all possibility. But the exploitative nature of a Rinehart world flies in the face of his southern background and its communal ethos. Yet, though the Hero has now questioned both the Brotherhood and Rinehart modes of existence, he does not yet accept the organizing of Blacks as being a human and interim way to effect real brotherhood. Hambro moves him in that direction. Explaining the injustice of his people being the sacrificial lamb for the Brotherhood's aims, the Hero is reminded that this is in fact the case in this instance, for the goals of the Brotherhood are vastly more important than the small dreams of blacks. Furthermore, he is told that blacks are not aggressive, that, in fact, they are inherently long-suffering. Therefore, any accommodation they would be required to make would certainly not be troublesome. The effect is that the invisible man embraces his past for the first time in more than an intuitive way, though this sober demysification of his history's distorted image serves to increase his emotional attachment to black people. He understands that he is the sum of his experiences, that they define him, and that those experiences are black. Thus, he returns to one of his most vivid memories, that of his grandfather's advice, and decides to "yassuh" the Brotherhood to destruction by agreeing with their long-suffering theory till Harlem boils over in their faces. A critical point here is that he desires to organize blacks and even believes great potential exists somewhere between Rinehart and invisibility, but knows that resources of all types are insufficient for victory.

The second event to strengthen his conversion is the Harlem riot. Depressed earlier because of inadequate resources to launch a splinter movement, he now exults in the supposition that blacks have effectively organized this rebellion on their own. As he moves into the crowd, he loses his individuality, becoming one with the masses. When he discovers that the Brotherhood has planned it by relinquishing their influence to Ras, he still demonstrates his racial solidarity, first by trying to convince Ras of the plan and then attempting to persuade the crowd. Failing both, yet recognizing himself as a leader of the people, he chooses to live out his own absurdity, deeming his grandfather's advice as either horribly mistaken or outdated. Destroying Jack is his next strategy, but as he moves to effect this, he is harassed by two whites who demand to know about the contents of his briefcase — his history. Outraged, he flees his accosters, still running toward Jack. The accidental fall underground may be all that prevents either his destruction or Jack's.

Underground, the Hero returns yet a last time to his grandfather's advice as well as to the absurdity of others in his historical notion of social obligation. Having dismissed the Brotherhood, Ras, and even violence — all carrying nationalistic implications — as the system to end black oppression, he seizes upon a fourth approach in a new interpretation of the old counsel. Now its meaning is to affirm the principle of democracy. Affirm the principle because blacks have lived it longer, even when it had another name in Africa; because they were forced to continue its practice here even in the face of being oppressed in its honor, since none other met their needs; and because they are connected to oppressed people everywhere. Yes, and for all their reasons, even affirm the principle for the oppressors, that they may secure a chance to be saved with the oppressed.

Here is a nationalism that recognizes its indispensableness to black survival in America, and that recognizes nationalism is narrow if it does not have as its final ambition that Brotherhood of all people. In addition, it is a nationalism which anticipates the civil rights movement when blacks dramatized the historically-felt responsibility to demonstrate the principle to those who had only professed it. And also, like the ideology of blacks involved in that movement, it is a nationalism that espouses cultural pluralism. In the Hero's words, "Our fate is to become one, yet many."[1]

Above-ground, I believe that the invisible man will remember his lessons in nationalism — those of the Brotherhood, Ras, and the violent impulse to destroy Jack and what he represented. But I also believe that he will use his demystification of the black past, and thus the black present, as well as a new grasp of his identity and black community values, to organize blacks for as long or short an interim necessary to usher in universal Brotherhood.

VI

Someplace to be
a Black Girl

If growing up is painful for the Southern black girl, being aware of her displace-
ment is the rust on the razor that threatens the throat.[1]

The Black female is assaulted in her tender years by all those common forces of
nature at the same time that she is caught in the tripartite crossfire of masculine
prejudice, white illogical hate and Black lack of power. The fact that the adult
American Negro female emerges a formidable character is often met with amaze-
ment, distaste and even belligerence. It is seldom accepted as an inevitable out-
come of the struggle won by survivors.[2]

These two statements from Maya Angelou's *I Know Why The Caged
Bird Sings* reflect the dilemma of Ms. Angelou's girlhood and the way that
she forged out of that dilemma. The first part of a series, this
autobiographical installment traces her development from a girl of three
in Stamps, Arkansas to a woman of almost seventeen with a baby boy in
San Francisco, California. And it is the early development of a black
female "Invictus" who is becoming the master of her fate and the captain
of her soul by the end of this phase of her life. She is discovering who she
is in spite of the forms of masculine prejudice, white illogical hate and
black lack of power with which she has been besieged. The most critical
masculine prejudice with which she was confronted was that in the eyes
of black boys — eyes persuaded by young minds already affected by the
colonizer's definitions that hourglass figures were the only ones with
which to pass the time of day, and that fair skin, straight hair, a slender
nose and thin lips were requisites for beauty. And though she is not yet in
favor with her own eyes by the time she brings two more male eyes into

the world, she is not obsessed with looking like white girls. The illogical hate of whites was ripe in Stamps and real in San Francisco, but she has refused to accommodate the power reverberations of that hate. Albeit she lived with black lack of power, it has not possessed her being. She has accepted neither whites controlling the lives of African-Americans nor African-Americans surrendering theirs. Thus, from a narrow crack in that small southern town and an ostensibly wider one in that large western city — St. Louis, Los Angeles and Mexico in between — she wedged a space, someplace to be a black girl. Marguerite Johnson — even though the painful process of maturation for a black girl in the South was intensified by her awareness that she had been assigned a place of no place — inevitably created a "place to be somebody," for she was a survivor.

To discover how Marguerite created someplace to be a black girl, we shall examine how she took the book world she gained access to and superimposed it on the overlapping yet distant black and white worlds in Stamps. Further, we shall analyze how she increasingly expanded the world she integrated from those first three by using the expanding space of societal permission and societal contact in her experience after Stamps. Marguerite "always, but ever and ever, thought that life was just one great risk for the living,"[3] and so took risks, disguised and open ones, in order to be. The freedom of the book world was too sweet not to transfer to the breathing ones.

Although Marguerite had already located the book world in print, it was Mrs. Bertha Flowers who set it securely on the axis of human communication. With the real world run by whites — a world with scarce black-white contact, much less communication — Mrs. Flowers' revelation that books could be rounded into a Third World provided a place much more livable than Stamps. Marguerite explains the meaning of the secret world furnished by Mrs. Flowers:

> To be allowed, no, invited, into the private lives of strangers and to share their joys and fears, was chance to exchange the Southern bitter wormwood for a cup of mead with Beowolf or a hot cup of tea and milk with Oliver Twist.[4]

The book world was a world of integration, where you were the confidant of all the denizens — in whose skins, regardless of color, you could move inside and breathe free. Yes, the black Dunbar, Hughes, Johnson and DuBois lived in that world, but so did the white Shakespeare, Kipling, Poe, Butler, Thackeray, and Henley. She saved her "young and loyal passion"[5] for the black writers, but she discovered ways to enjoy the company of white writers who related to her real world. It "was Shakespeare who said, 'When in disgrace with fortune and men's eyes',"[6] a condition she identified with when she thought about her plight in Stamps, a young castaway without parents in a freedom-stifling, small southern town. The statement also fit her estimate of herself in the eyes of people, especially young black boys. Shakespeare sympathized with the "black, ugly dream"[7] that was her existence, and so became her "first white love."[8] She rationalized her courtship "by saying that after all he had been dead so long it couldn't matter to anyone any more."[9] The "beautiful sad lines" of "Annabel Lee" appertained to the sadness of her life "stalled by the South and Southern Black lifestyle."[10] And whether it was the comic strips, cowboy books or Horatio Alger, she craved another space, a place to be a happy black girl. The freedom of the cowboys, "the strong heroes who always conquered in the end,"[11] and the penniless shoeshine boys who, with goodness and perseverance, became rich, rich men and gave baskets of goodies to the poor on holidays, became more real than the people in her haltingly moving space. Tiny Tim was her favorite on "Sunday as he eluded the evil men and bounded back from each seeming defeat as sweet and gentle as ever."[12] As she daydreamed herself into fortune and the grace of men's eyes, she identified with "the little princesses who were mistaken for maids, and the long-lost children mistaken for waifs."[13] Marguerite refused to restrict her life to the world of the cotton fields; like her father, Bailey Sr., she had "aspirations of grandeur."[14] And it was this survivor spirit that impelled her to turn her mind fast enough to occupy a less confining globe.

Marguerite Johnson banished segregation in her book world, and she wanted no part of her culture that she associated with powerlessness in the world of book learning. Considered stuck-up by her schoolmates, she took pride in the school principal's proper English and tailored her speech accordingly, speech free of what she considered the rough edges of a "Southern accent" or "common slang."[15] In fact, one of her most traumatic experiences was graduation from the eighth grade at Lafayette County Training School. The long anticipated event was ruined by a combination of the white arrogance of the commencement speaker, Mr. Donleavy, and the apparent acceptance by African-Americans in the audience that they could only aspire to be great athletes. Education was supposed to be the exit out of the stultifying South, and now a white man was saying that they should try to emulate only the "Jesse Owenses and Joe Louises."[16] Enraged by the presumptuousness and rebutting each sentence, she wondered "what school official in the white-goddom of Little Rock had the right to decide that these two men must be our only heroes."[17] Further, she willed instant death to the black owner of the first Amen, hoping that he/she would choke on the word. She also considered the recitation of "Invictus" by Elouise, the daughter of the Baptist minister, impertinent, and was aggravated by Henry Reed's valedictory address, "To Be or Not to Be." If according to Mr. Donleavy — who represented all whites — African-Americans could not be, and Whites were the masters of their fate and the captain of their souls, then commencement was just another exercise in futility. "We were maids and farmers, handymen and washerwomen, and anything higher that we aspired to was farcical and presumptuous."[18] If education was not a way out of the strictures of the Stamps in this country, then democracy was a sham, and all the people, black and white, who were regarded as contributors to that cause, had lived in vain. It would have been preferable for everyone to have died than continue to play out this "ancient tragedy"[19] of white power and black impotence. Marguerite summarizes the feelings that characterized her attitude about being denied self-determination:

> It was awful to be Negro and have no control over my life. It was brutal to be young and already trained to sit quietly and listen to charges brought against my color with no chance of defense.[20]

It was only when Henry Reed, class valedictorian, began to lead the class and then the black audience in the Negro National Anthem — which had been struck from its customary place to remove the risk of offending the speaker and his white companion — that Marguerite sensed the strength and the pride of black people. Although she had sung the words thousands of times, she "had never heard it before...never thought they (words) had anything to do with me."[21] And so black writers assumed a new dimension. They were not only kindred souls in the free book world, but they enlarged the space in the real one by expanding the spirit until one felt the very power. For the first time, the Anthem carried as much a freedom message as had Patrick Henry's words, "I know not what course others may take, but as for me, give me liberty or give me death." For the first time, Marguerite recognized how black writers not only made possible an alternative world, but pushed the boundaries outward in her actual world:

> Oh, Black known and unknown poets, how often have your auctioned pains sustained us? Who will compute the lonely nights made less lonely by your songs, or the empty pots made less tragic by your tales? [22]

Perhaps, for Marguerite, who could abide no indication of weakness in her people, this was the most useful lesson of those eight years. Mr. Donleavy had unwittingly helped her to demystify her ideas about the power of education for powerless African-Americans, but a racial and literary ancestor had afforded her the strength to resist his dehumanization. Only the strong survive!

Now that we have established some measurement of Marguerite's book world, we need to investigate her ideas of the two living worlds — black and white — that she wished to coincide with the paper one. We need to ascertain what qualities in both worlds were so undesirable that she felt compelled to fit another world on them to oppose her dehumanization. First, however, it is important that we know how she did identify with the black world in Stamps. Marguerite's strongest identification with black people was with their independence, their desire and ability to be free from the control of whites. Although she commiserated with their abject conditions in Stamps, she wanted them to abide their poverty with a straight spine.[23]

All of the black people that she admired possessed some degree of freedom from whites. Momma Johnson, her grandmother, owned a store which whites patronized, owned land and houses, and "had more money than all the powhitetrash."[24] In fact, she lent money to whites, including the dentist, during the Depression. Marguerite "knew that there were a number of white folks in town that owed her favors."[25] So Momma was a black woman to look up to, who not only was "the only Negro woman in Stamps referred to once as Mrs."[26] — though by error — but who also asserted herself and won strange victories over both poor white girls and a rich white man — the dentist.

In the store, Momma sidestepped servility with the "powhitetrash girls" by anticipating their needs and thus obviating their orders. Outside the store on one memorable occasion, she was heckled by the girls but stood her ground quietly with the moan-song of old black Christian warriors in her throat even when they subjected her to the indignity of indignities — having one of their gang expose her genitals by doing a hand-stand without underwear. Even though Marguerite could not fathom why her grandmother did not come inside to avoid such humiliation, she realized, after the ordeal, that "whatever the contest had been out front,...Momma had won."[27]

Momma also won the bout with Dentist Lincoln, who had never treated a black patient. She pleaded with him to extract two of Marguerite's teeth, reminding him that she had once lent him money, but he refused, saying that he would rather stick his "hand in a dog's mouth than a nigger's."[28] Marguerite remembered how she had been dismissed by Momma, and how she had imagined a scene between Momma and the dentist and his nurse. In that scene, Momma, with "well enunciated"[29] words, castigated the dentist, ordered him out of Stamps, relegated him to a veterinarian, and refused to waste the energy to kill him. When leaving, "she waved her handkerchief at the nurse and turned her into a crocus sack of chicken feed."[30]

Mr. McElroy and Mrs. Flowers were two mysterious black adults whom Marguerite admired because they also seemed to control their own lives. Mr. McElroy was the only black man that she "knew, except for the school principal and the visiting teachers, who wore matching pants and jackets....A man who owned his land and the big many-windowed house with a porch that clung to its sides all around the house. An independent Black man."[31] Mrs. Flowers, patron saint who had helped her retrieve her dignity with books and thus her ability to speak after she had been silenced by the rape of her stepfather, "was the aristocrat of Black Stamps."[32] The rape rendered her powerless and reduced her beneath dignity. She could not speak until she regained her dignity; she could not regain her dignity until she recovered her power. Mrs. Flowers was the agent of her empowerment and epitomized dignity:

> Like women in English novels who walked the moors (whatever they were) with their loyal dogs racing at a respectful distance. Like the women who sat in front of roaring fireplaces, drinking tea incessantly from silver trays full of scones and crumpets. Women who walked over the 'heath' and read morocco-bound books and had two last names divided by a hyphen. [33]

If this sounds like a young black girl in whiteface, we must remember that Marguerite's book world was a ready replacement for what often appeared to be a subjugated culture — black life in Stamps. Unwittingly, she drew her living models from the face of power, although both her hate of white dehumanization and her visceral belonging to the people that sometimes made her "a proud member of the wonderful, beautiful Negro race"[34] insisted that the owner of the face be black.

Joe Louis, the Brown Bomber, wore a black face, and held the fists of almost all black people in his hands when he stepped into the ring to not only defend his heavyweight championship but his people. Marguerite was one of his people, one of the black ritual participants in the late Thirties on the nights of the Louis fights. She remembered how the community gathered and waited on the radio to bring the news of another Louis victory — a black victory. And it wasn't only Carnera on the canvass; it was all white people. And then Marguerite was proud to belong to her people, because Joe Louis was the "champion of the world. A Black boy. Some Black mother's son...the strongest man in the world."[35] So Marguerite belonged to the strongest people in the world, at least for a while.

Marguerite carried other black heroes on the shoulders of her mind when they seemed to live free of white clutches. When Bailey Sr., her father, came to Stamps, she was "so proud of him it was hard to wait for the gossip to get around that he was in town."[36] Why? He spoke "proper English, like the school principal, and even better....Every one could tell from the way he talked and from the car (De Soto) and clothes that he was rich and maybe had a castle out in California."[37] Marguerite needed exemplars of what she considered freedom to believe in the possibility of her own. Although, as we shall see, she became more secure in her identity as her real world expanded beyond Stamps, she was thrilled by the fact that her uncles in St. Louis whipped whites as well as African-Americans and that the black underground men in San Francisco made fortunes from "the wealthy bigoted whites, and in every case...used the victims' prejudice against them."[38]

If independence in the black world of Stamps was the most important quality contributing to Marguerite's identification with black people, subordination was so unbearable that she could not keep full residency in that world. She allied emotionally with her community, with their ordeals in cotton fields, in "rivers of blood," and with white noses in the sky. But, it was the fire of black reaction that she wanted; "no more water, the fire next time." Part of her early rejection of southern black culture — her avoiding the common slang and her wanting others to think that she had to be forced to eat black cuisine — was because she associated those things with the powerlessness of black people.

No matter which blacks in Stamps exhibited what Marguerite deemed approval of white dehumanization or characteristics that she related to black powerlessness, she disclaimed their behavior. She made no exceptions. Even her grandmother and her crippled son, Uncle Willie, whom she loved dearly, chafed her when they seemed to tolerate white humiliation. Momma warmed her under her wings in many ways — for which Marguerite was always grateful — but she did not understand why Momma permitted the "powhitetrash" girls to be disrespectful to her in her own store, using her first name. And until Marguerite was quieted by her and convinced by her smiling face that somehow the girls had lost that pitched battle of humiliation outside the store, she was enraged that Momma, who owned the land that the girls lived on, allowed them to affront her with a display of nakedness. She describes the aftermath:

> I burst. A firecracker July-the-Fourth burst. How could Momma call them Miz? The mean nasty things...What did she prove? And then if they were dirty, mean and impudent, why did Momma have to call them Miz?[39]

Marguerite wanted to shoot the girls with "the 410, our sawed-off shotgun behind the screen door."[40] And until she had been dismissed by her grandmother from the private office of the insulting Dr. Lincoln — a dismissal that she construed as a sign that her grandmother was going to bless out the white dentist — Marguerite had been angry with Momma for describing "herself as if she had no last name to the young white nurse"[41] who answered the back door and closed it firmly in their faces. Her handicapped Uncle Willie managed no more sympathy when he tolerated the "powhitetrash" children's calling him by his first name, and he mortified her by obeying their orders "in his limping dip-straight-dip fashion."[42]

Outside her family, Marguerite was no more understanding of African-Americans following Southern protocol or sympathetic to their efforts to wrest meaning from life if they seemed accommodative to whites. Although Marguerite was an integral part of Southern black rituals and a firsthand witness to the atrocities that shaped those rituals, she expected the miracle of the spirit to raise the living bones. During the perturbations of the graduation exercises mentioned earlier, she castigated all African-Americans who did not appear to be incensed by the racism of Donleavy's remarks. And although she sympathized with the cotton pickers who stopped at Momma's store for physical and spiritual sustenance, "had seen the fingers cut by the mean little cotton bolls, and...had witnessed the backs and shoulders and arms and legs resisting any further demands,"[43] she insisted that they rise:

> I thought them all hateful to have allowed themselves to be worked like oxen, and even more shameful to try to pretend that things were not as bad as they were. When they leaned too hard on the partly glass candy counter, I wanted to tell them shortly to stand up and 'assume the posture of a man.'[44]

And although Marguerite was taken to the annual revivals by Momma, and interpreted the happiness on the black faces and their verbal participations in the sermons of the evangelists as satisfaction "that they were going to be the only inhabitants of that land of milk and honey, except of course a few white folks like John Brown,"[45] she watched them after the benediction, and thought that "outside and on the way home, the people played in their magic as children poke in mud pies, reluctant to tell themselves that the game was over."[46]

Marguerite never accepted the occlusions of her place as a black girl in the white South. In thought, word and deed, she pushed against them, making soft spots and then fissures. When "the used-to-be sheriff" rode up to the store late one day and warned Momma to hide Uncle Willie, because the Klan would be by later to avenge the behavior of "a crazy nigger (who) messed with a white lady today,"[47] Marguerite pledged that not even St. Peter would secure a testimony from her that the act had been kind. She detested "his confidence that my uncle and every other Black man who heard of the Klan's coming ride would scurry under their houses to hide in chicken droppings."[48] When the "powhitetrash children," who did not obey the customary laws of being respectful, "took liberties in my store that I would never dare,"[49] she pinched them, "partly out of angry frustration."[50] Marguerite's experiences in St. Louis with "the numbers runners, gamblers, lottery takers and whiskey salesmen" waiting in the living room of her mother's mother for favors, and with the Syrian brothers at Louie's tavern competing for her mother's attention because she approximated white beauty standards, were sources of new models of black female strength for her return to Stamps as well as of reinforced mystification about her appearance. And so she was more likely than ever to resist the violations of her space as a human being, although she was only able to shift her center of gravity regarding her beauty from white to high yellow. Thus later in Stamps, when she worked in the kitchen of a white woman, Mrs. Viola Cullinan, who insisted on abbreviating her name to Mary, Marguerite reacted to being "called out of her name" by dropping Mrs. Cullinan's favorite dishware, "a casserole shaped like a fish and the green glass coffee cups."[51] Yet, when watching a Kay Francis movie from the Negro balcony, she not only dismissed the obsequious behavior of Kay's black maid and chauffeur as beneath her dignity, but she answered the white laughter at such behavior with her own, reveling in the fact of "white folks" not knowing that the woman they were adoring could be my mother's twin, except that she was white and my mother was prettier."[52]

Marguerite used the expanded possibilities of the world after Stamps to further enlarge her world. In Stamps, she had to create a world of freedom — a place to be a black girl — in her book world, in her identification with Blacks who seemed independent of white strictures, in her refusal to identify with Blacks who stayed in their white-determined places, and in her resistance to white dictation and dehumanization. In San Francisco, for "a thirteen-year old Black girl, stalled by the South and Southern Black life style, the city was a state of beauty and a state of freedom."[53] And yet, in spite of a Miss Kirwin, a brilliant teacher at George Washington High School who, as Mrs. Flowers, acknowledged her place in the world "for just being Marguerite Johnson;" and a month-long experience in a junkyard car home with whites, as well as Mexicans and other Blacks — which demonstrated the possibilities of human harmony with places and spaces enough for everyone — she saw the unmistakable evidence of racism:

> San Francisco would have sworn on the Golden Gate Bridge that racism was missing from the heart of their air-conditioned city. But they would have been sadly mistaken.[54]

Not only were there stories of racism that went the rounds, but there were the realities. Marguerite imbibed the stories of her stepfather's friends about the prejudices of wealthy, bigoted whites being exploited by black con men as tonic for the more subtle Northern symptoms of the disease. But concrete racism could only be tempered by concrete resistance. And so, when at fifteen, she decided to pursue the career of a streetcar operator, only to be informed by her mother that colored people were not accepted on streetcars, Marguerite once again found it necessary to stretch her tall resistance to make room for her spirit. After initially forgiving the white receptionist at Market Street Railway Company for protecting the bastion of white supremacy with the niceties of ritualistic circumventions, even accepting "her as a fellow victim of the same puppeteer"[55] who denied her and her people places to be somebody, she was awakened from her meditation that "the miserable little encounter had nothing to do with me, the me of me, any more than it had to do with that silly clerk"[56] by the "Southern nasal accent (and) usual hard eyes of white contempt"[57] of the conductorette on her way home. Marguerite brought her South up North, where it belonged, realizing that racism was no respecter of geography:

> All lies, all comfortable lies. The receptionist was not innocent and neither was I. The whole charade we had played out in that crummy waiting room had directly to do with me, Black, and her, white.[58]

Marguerite Johnson persisted in her resistance to the thumbnail place of black girls in the South, in the anywhere. She became "the first Negro on the San Francisco streetcars."[59] She could not like the "fate to live the poorest, roughest life;"[60] she could not "bear the heavy burden of Blackness"[61] that required her to balance dehumanization on even the back of the mind; she had "to be or not to be." Marguerite, in her book world that she opposed to the white world, in her black world that she opposed to the hue man world, survived and began to center her marginalized status, moving toward the myths of black identity and black ethos. She was a poet of the spirit who knew that internal rhyme was as beautiful as end rhyme, perhaps one and the same. As she said at twelve:

> If we were a people much given to revealing secrets, we might raise monuments and sacrifices to the memories of our poets, but slavery cured us of that weakness. It may be enough, however, to have it said that we survive in exact relationship to the dedication of our poets (including preachers, musicians and blues singers).[62]

Include Marguerite!

Coming Out of Colonization:
The Cotillion

Unlike Ralph Ellison, John O. Killens has not only accepted the politics of all literature, but has also openly argued the indispensability of correct politics for African-American literature. Unlike Richard Wright, Killens' correct politics calls for a hold on transcending nationalism until the prospects for universalism are black brighter. He recognizes that "we black folk are a colony on the mainland"[1] and that the black writer must address that reality as long as it is true. Killens' novel *The Cotillion* is a masterful effort in reflecting the mystifying and dehumanizing effects of the colonizer's cultural repression as well as colonized resistance. A "black comedy...halfly autobiographical and halfly fiction,"[2] it raises serious questions about the identity and values of some "brothers and sisters of the middle-class repression"[3] and the countervailing forces of black consciousness. Set in Harlem and in Brooklyn, the "writer," Ben Ali Lumumba, focuses on "a fox named Yoruba"[4] whom he helps to struggle with her great ambivalence: the battle that raged "inside of her between her mother and her father, between ladyship and womanhood. The confrontation black and white."[5] In order to understand this tension in Yoruba, it is necessary to first examine the characterizations of her mother and father, Daphne and Matthew Lovejoy, before the cotillion invitation.

Daphne Doreen Braithwaite Lovejoy epitomizes E. Franklin Frazier's black bourgeoisie and Nathan Hare's Black Anglo-Saxon, although she is not middle-class. Having worked up from being a maid for whites to becoming a housewife in a three room-and-bath apartment in Harlem, she plans to continue moving on up by consorting with black elites from Brooklyn. Her association with black women in the Episcopal church finally pays off when her daughter Yoruba is invited by their social group, Femmes Fatales, to be one of five Harlem "culturally deprived" girls to "integrate" their cotillion. To be sure, this is the realization of her life's dream.

But to really understand Daphne, we must reckon with the reality of her early life. Born in Christ Church in Barbados — Little England, according to Daphne — to one of eleven concubines of her Scottish father, Squire Angus Braithwaite, she is confronted very early by colonial realities and definitions that mystify her experience. Finally revealing her young years to Yoruba, she explains her cultural duality:

> You young folks talk about dignity now. Well, I wanted dignity bad. I saw that the white man had all the pride and dignity in the world. My mother and her folks was the humble people. Wherever my white father walked, Black men bowed and scraped, so I despised the Black in me.[6]

Not only did Daphne then begin to identify with the colonizer's values, but with his physical features as well. In that same exchange with Yoruba, she recounts an early incident in Jamaica when she was ten, when a blind aunt described her, after patting her on the head, as the black one with the wooly head:

> I cried. I ran and looked into the looking glass. I was as fair as Goldilocks and I had a bad grade of good hair, or a good grade of bad hair, whichever. And I cried, I wanted to be white. And if I ever had any children I prayed to God they would be white, or I would do everything to make them white. [7]

That incident with her aunt became the basis for both Daphne's own identity as a black woman as well as for her struggle to fashion Yoruba into a colored beauty. Although Daphne had used the mirror before the trauma to remind herself that she almost met the beauty standard she unwittingly accepted, afterwards, the looking-glass affirmation ritual became a fixation. She "never passed a mirror without staring admiringly into it,"[8] reassuring herself of her slender upturned nose, thin mouth, bluish-green eyes, and skin that was "perhaps a little duskier than ordinary Western queens."[9] And when she looked at Yoruba, she saw "a beautiful girl, despite the fact that she inherited her father's color and his looks."[10] Approving especially Yoruba's high cheekbones and slender upturned nose, Daphne would reflect on her struggle to mold her little girl into a thing of beauty:

> How she used to make the girl pull her lips in and keep them in when she was a baby, so they would grow thin and slender (she used to say 'aquiline' till she looked the word up in the dictionary). How she used to keep her away from the beaches and off the streets out of the sunlight, and never let the girl drink coffee, which would make her Blacker than she already was. [11]

Ironically, it was these same early years in Barbados that provided the wedge into Daphne's blackness later. After coming to New York, she tells Yoruba why she did not marry a white man:

> Because every white man I met in this country had no respect for me. All of them had one thing in mind. And I swear a long time ago, I kissed the Good Book, that I ain't never be the white man's whore...Or his concubine like my mother was. [12]

Until Daphne works the white cotillion — which shall be detailed later — she nonetheless attempts to do everything to make Yoruba white. Her Barbadian observation about the colonizer having all the pride and dignity in the world was buttressed by what she saw here. And so, her desire to be, to have access to pride and dignity, seemed to lead to no true fruition. She lives a lie, "worshipping the memory of my father, a white man who look upon me as one of his pickaninnies." [13] She has to hold onto something, even if it isn't real.

Thus until the white cotillion, Daphne's reinforced mystification in this country is clearly reflected in her attitudes and behavior as mother of the single child, Yoruba, and wife to the dark-skinned Matt. Her repeated references to Great Britain as the mother country and to Barbados as "Little England" demonstrate her identification with whites and their power. Not only was she a "Scotch American...who thought that, with a little luck and a slight assist from the Great-One-Up-On-High, she might have been the Queen of England," [14] but sometimes in her delirium, she became an Englishwoman. As one of the "first-family" coloreds in Barbados who was "comfortably confident that Britons would never be slaves," [15] and who could weep at the sound of "God Save the Queen" and "Rule Britannia," Daphne was capable of imaginatively joining the ranks of the colonizer when nostalgically remembering Barbados, the home of "'The Last of the Unspoiled Peoples' (with) everybody living the life of Riley in the big mansions with a staff of splendid servants waiting on them hands and feet."[16] As she explains to Lumumba that the natives are happy and contented, she becomes one with the colonizer, warning against the prospect of revolution:

> If the damn worthless peace-loving cane-cutting natives git some notions in their head we'll show them as long as Britannia rules the waves, after all the dear Queen is done for them, damn their Black contented souls! By Christ, we will not stand for violence. We'll blow that happy little island off the map.[17]

By extension, Daphne's identification with the colonizer's power in Barbados led to her obsession with integration in this country and to her association with the Femmes Fatales. In fact, Yoruba's invitation to the cotillion was but the latest step in Daphne's relentless climb toward the citadel of white power and her dignity. In the Brooklyn Memorial Episcopal Cathedral, she had sought out and discovered Mrs. Patterson, the condescending but sympathetic bourgeois spirit that reached down to lift as she climbed. And so, Yoruba was on her way up to a Sarah Lawrence, Smith, or Radcliffe education to snare a near-white husband and to live in a blessed integrated neighborhood where you were awakened every morning by the heavenly music of chimes.

Daphne's false moorings would probably have anchored Yoruba early in black disaffection, had it not been for the counterpoise of her father Matt. Although she had witnessed her mother's repeated excoriations of her father's black pride, and was told by Daphne that she had made a mistake in marrying Matt, Yoruba sensed solidity in the marriage. In spite of her mother's outbursts, he was quietly firm, and she guessed that Daphne secretly admired his strength. Most of all, Matt remained proud, and it was contagious. Even before Yoruba met Lumumba, her father had helped her to demystify the experience of being black, and thus had been a factor in her resistance of the dehumanizing forces of her mother's tutelage.

Born in Georgia, Matthew Lovejoy came to Harlem in 1928, a country boy whose city finesse was even shorter than the pants that he wore. Although his cousin said he was so green that he smelled like collard greens, Matt brought a rich boyhood of black southern ways with him: getting religion, "signs and haints and spirits, goofy dust and all that stuff. Working roots and conjure-men. Rabbit feet and black cat bones."[18] H e brought that education and the great American dream with him. Graduating from the "University of Hard Knocks and Disappointments,"[19] he had pushed his way up from waiting tables to becoming a redcap at the Pennsylvania Station. In between, he had tried his hand at business — including several restaurants — but his African heart had been too soft to win at free enter-prise. Regularly, he gave too many starving people "credick."

Matt Lovejoy was a black man, mythic in black identity and ethos. Not only was he "black unwrinkled velvet...(with) large lips, nostrils, eyes, (and) wide forehead,"[20] but he also anchored his roots in Africa, "all the way to Arachuku, that land of fable of the long juju."[21] Remembering black slavery in this country as he sweated to make a living, he sometimes thought that "maybe I worked way back yonder in slavery time. Maybe I'm the second coming of old Nat Turner and Frederick Douglass put together and multiplied."[22]

Yet Matt, in spite of his lift-to-can't-lift labor, found time to dream of Africa's past and his future in his chair-of-chairs at home or Jenkins Palace Barbershop: "Someday, somehow, sometime, a change was gonna come. Yeah — he was going to overcome. Dream of Africa and all its ancient glory."[23]

Not only had Matt "made his pilgrimage to Timbuktu so many times in so many of his dreams,...entered barefoot at the mosque,...(and) studied at the ancient university,"[24] but he had consistently worked in Harlem for the realization of the dream of Africa's future after he relinquished the American dream:

> Matt had taken up the banner of his blackness and carried it unfurled all the way from Garvey to Malcolm. Matt had marched behind every Black man who ever raised his voice in Harlem, including Garvey, Powell, Ben Davis, Paul Robeson, and very very naturally, Brother Malcolm.[25]

Of course, the center of Matthew Lovejoy's dream of Africa's future was his daughter. And so from his "Black and wondrously angry and terribly frustrated nationalism,"[26] Matt named his only child Yoruba. (Daphne, in true fashion, added Evelyn, and called her Ruby or Eve.) Tracing his history to Africa, he would tell Yoruba that "her skin was like it had been scrubbed with fine stones from the River Niger."[27] Matt deflected Daphne's attacks on Yoruba's childhood ghetto friends, and he paralyzed Daphne each night after work when he would put Yoruba "on his shoulders with her legs around his neck and ride her all the way up the block and into the house."[28] Daphne labelled them both "just as common as all the other no-good darkies in this ratty neighborhood."[29] For Matt and Yoruba, "it was the happiest moment in the day for both of them."[30] They labelled it love.

Matt loved black life: black music and dance, black women, black food, black camaraderie of the barbershop, and black religion. As soon as he borrowed some urban wisdom from his reckless cousin, Matt introduced himself to black sporting life. He whooped it up uptown stomping at the Savoy Ballroom, and "fell in and out of love (and by the numbers) with each of the dance-for-pay girls."[31] In fact, he met Daphne at the Savoy, "met her on a Thursday night, which was ladies night, a night when women came in free of charge. It was the night-out for New York's sleep-in 'kitchen mechanics'." [32] Daphne ended his love affairs, but not his love for music; Matt learned all the black dances he did not know, including West Indian ones. Daphne, through trial and error, learned how to please his palate with a mixture of Southern and West Indian cuisine, but did not cater to his predilection for black religion. Matt wanted no part of the Brooklyn Memorial Episcopal Cathedral, the white Father Madison Mayfair of that sanctuary in Crowning Heights that had become black in the last ten years, the genuflection, and was not too particular about the high-class colored parishioners. Matt's Jesus, as he would argue in the barbershop, was a Black Power man, and he could not understand all those black sheep, especially his wife, having a white shepherd:

> Damn if that don't beat everything. Calling a white man Father in these days and
> times. Father May-damn-fair. Everybody everywhere else in the world busy as a
> cat covering up shit trying their best to get rid of all the Great White Fathers, and
> y'all paying that sissyass pimp to help y'all get in the white man's heaven, where
> they gon have all you Negroes doing days work anyhow. Cooking, scrubbing, and
> carrying on.[33]

Matt Lovejoy was not an idolizer of white men. He explains his expertise on them to Daphne: "I know the white man cause I done handled all his baggage... I know what the white man putting down, cause I been picking it up for almost thirty years, and long before."[34]

He did not counsel turning the other cheek either in confrontations with them. As he told his comrades in the barbershop, "if the rabbits took rock-throwing lessons, there wouldn't be all them many hunters pitching boogie in the forest."[35]

Yoruba had been caught in this crisscross fire of identity and values between her father and mother long before she was invited to the cotillion. Although she knew that she was loved and recognized their love for each other in the interstices of their differences, she had often found herself betwixt and between. She had her father's approval of her poor playmates when she was a girl; her mother labelled them "low-class darkies,"[36] trying both to persuade Yoruba that they were her inferiors and to break up the associations. She loved her father's piggyback rides, but her mother would scold her for not acting like a lady. Her father thought that she was beautiful; her mother kept trying to repair her beauty. Her mother tugged her to the elitist black church; her father refused to join. She, as her father, liked Ellington, as well as calypso, and rock 'n' roll; her mother hated that "common nigger music from the streets."[37] Her father followed Malcolm, and she had been in love with him; her mother continued to sing the praises of Squire Angus Braithwaite, Scottish sugar plantation and rum distillery owner in Barbados, and also her father. Push and pull. Pull and push.

Actually, Yoruba was leaning blackly when the reader meets her at eighteen. "For the last fifteen or eighteen months, she had lived a life, whenever she was outside her home, or away from school, or job, in a world of total blackness."[38] But she discovered that for others, much of it was a game where slogans, trappings, capitalistic ventures, and male requests of sexual favors represented the extent of the revolution. Even Yoruba, who was no player of games, would occasionally get caught up in the fashion of blackness, and urge her mother to get out in the sun more often so that she would not be mistaken for white. But then she "would realize what she was doing to her mother, vicious thing, and feel guilty at the doing of it."[39] Ironically, it was another physical feature, hair, that was pulling Yoruba away from accepting her own blackness:

She had gone all the way with the Black thing, except that she had not cut off the long black stuff that crowned her head with shining glory and spilled down to her shoulders in sweet black cascades.[40]

And now the Great Debate — the Cotillion. Now, Yoruba had to turn inside to see where this tug of war had left her. She wondered how far she was from the terrible line that marked victory for colonial dehumanization:

> How do you tell your mother you don't want to be a lady? That you would rather be a good Black woman? The truth of the matter, there was this great ambivalence in the girl.[41]

Her father thought it ridiculous to spend half a grand — which they would have to borrow — for one night at the Waldorf, but said that he would support her decision, cotillion or no; her mother insisted that it would be the beginning of heaven on earth. Even before the climactic argument, she felt the yank of the dominant culture: "Against her will she did feel a kind of triumph that she had been selected. She, Yoruba, was to be a debutante. What was wrong with feeling good about it? "[42]

Her mother's tears gave her even less sure footing; perhaps she could lie, agree to the cotillion, and yet hold the line. But then, perhaps, she did not have to lie to hold the line:

> Just who was she to be scornful of the Grand Cotillion? Out of all the thousands of girls in Harlem, she had been one of five selected. She was proud and grateful. She had something to look forward to.[43]

Without the strong force of her father's opposition, and on the slippery terrain of her feelings for her mother and her feelings about the cotillion, Yoruba edges toward the dehumanizing demarcation of colonial definitions by agreeing to be a debutante. Enter Lumumba, another graduate of the "University of Hard Knocks and Disappointments," with his rap of colonial degradation, his own ambivalences, but finally with the hand that helped her father pull her hemp across the line away from dehumanization and her mother.

Ben Ali Lumumba — alias Ernest Walter Billings, nose-picking, thumb-sucking, puppy-lover of Yoruba when she was about six — reenters her life "in the très hip Cafe Uptown Society of the hip Black people."[44] She does not recognize him as her ragged black prince of yesteryear — a "common low-class Southern nigger"[45] to her mother — who disappeared when his mother died. But Yoruba, who wanted to try her own heart at poetry, does recognize and is enamored by "his poetic thing in the 'Roi-Jones-Dante-Graham-Archie-Shepp-Askia Muhammed-Toure fashion,"[46] as Lumumba raps his revolutionary poetry. After cutting through his postiche approach, the approach of Lumumba the womanizer, she discovers the real black man whose eyes settle the question of her beauty, and whose insight helps to settle the question of the cotillion. By the time the preparations for the cotillion have reached the point of choosing an escort, Yoruba has grown so attached to him that she resists the temptation of asking someone from a bourgeois family and asks Lumumba. Lumumba, in turn, reinforces her father's notions about the inanity and danger of the cotillion, and enforces the legitimacy of black beauty standards in the space that they occupy.

Although Matthew had not forbidden Yoruba to accept the invitation to the cotillion, he had not minced words in explaining its meaning. He claimed that rich whites had learned long ago from cattle farming that one good bull was half the herd, and so had "invented these debitramp balls so that their darling little heifers could get a good shot at the prize bull in the pasture."[47] On the other hand, blacks were just imitating whites for the sake of being like them, unaware of their purposes, and suffering different consequences:

> But colored folks just do these things cause they see white folks doing them. It ain't no investment like it is with white folks. All the money ends up in Whitey's hands again. To the dance teacher, to the beauty peoples, to Mr. Waldorf. It's just some more white folks' foolishness that don't git Black folks nowheres except in debt. Like Santa Claus and Easter bonnets, it all ends up in Charlie's pockets.[48]

When Daphne calls him ignorant, suggesting that the Femmes Fatales were trying to uplift black people, Matthew rejoins that they were trying to abandon black people:

> They tryna run off and leave the Race and innergrate into the white folks. That's what the Grand-damn-cotillion is all about-to make little white sissies outa the colored educated boys and girls. Turn the cream of the crap against the poor Black people.[49]

Yoruba's demystification of the cotillion by her father is strengthened by Lumumba. Although he finally consented to be her escort — in part

95

because he was "afraid of open competition with those pretty, proper-talk-ing, prissy-assed, high yalla boys from the university"[50] — he echoes Matthew's warnings and adds new dimensions to the dangers of the cotil-lion. Telling Yoruba that black people will never be liberated by mimick-ing cultural symbols, he argues that the Femmes Fatales are unwitting enemy agents who work against a sense of black nationalism:

> The Grand Cotillion and all that other bourgeois bullshit are pulling Black folks
> in the opposite direction of peoplehood. The Cotillion says: 'You don't need no
> power. You don't need no peoplehood. You don't need to be no nation. You going
> to be integrated. You going to be just like white folks.'....Then damn cotillions mess
> up a whole heap of potentially beautiful Black heads, for days, Sheba. Every year
> some good black folks, young and future generation folks, get wasted, lost forever
> to themselves and to the Movement.[51]

The weeks of Yoruba's preparation for the cotillion further support the analysis of her father and Lumumba, as the artificiality of the lives of the Brooklyn bourgeoisie removes any vestige of the idea that being part of such a group represents progress. Even more important, however, is that the preparation raises to the surface Yoruba's uncertainty about her own beauty, an issue of dehumanization. The years of being reared by a mother who accepted the standards of European beauty as universal took its toll. Yoruba could not lightly dismiss memories of wearing clothespins to keep her nose thin, of repeatedly being scolded about not keeping her lips pulled in, and of being kept out of the sun and even prevented from drinking coffee because her mother believed that it would make her darker. Yet Yoruba's love for her father may have given her some pride in inheriting his full mouth and dark brown complexion closer to his than that of her mother, for she does not seem to be traumatized by Daphne's insistence that neither of them is black and that she does not hold Matthew's color against him. One conversation that Yoruba has with her mother after she has been invited to one of the Brooklyn bour-geois homes for dinner perhaps best delineates the struggle that she wages with her self-image. As Daphne revels in the invitation, singing the praise of the Brasswork family, she encourages Yoruba to make friends with the daughter, Brenda Brasswork, and then begins to glorify all of Brenda's physical features. She tells Yoruba that Brenda "could almost pass for white...and she's got good hair too. It's even better than mine."[52] Yoruba gets nowhere with the argument that all hair is good, and in the volatility of the exchange, she is moved to tears. She feels rejected; perhaps her innermost feelings about her own attractiveness can be found in her final response to Daphne:

> Okay, Mother, you win. Brassy Brenda is lovely, your daughter is ugly. Brassy Brenda is high yaller, your daughter's Black. Brassy Brenda got good hair, your daughter's hair is evil, bad, and terrible.[53]

Without Lumumba, Yoruba may have succumbed to the colonial definitions of beauty to which her mother subscribed. As mentioned earlier, her black pride before she met him had been insufficient for her to follow the lead of most black women in the late Sixties who were wearing Afros.

The preparation for the cotillion crystallizes Lumumba's salutary impact on Yoruba's self-image. His constant reminders of how beautiful she is to him bolsters her belief in her attractiveness to the point that she musters the courage to suggest to two of the other debutantes that they all wear their hair au naturel to the cotillion. This was a major step away from colonization, for she had secretly prided herself on at least having a "good grade of bad hair."[55] But as the day of beauty-parlor reckoning approached, she vacillated. "How would she look?...Would she be ugly? Would she be Black and comely?"[56] She admits her apprehension to Lumumba, but is persuaded by his eyes to go ahead:

> The way he looked at her now, as he stood there staring at her with love and worshipful adoration in his eyes, she knew her beauty, saw it in his penetrating eyes.... She was, in fact, the most beautiful woman in the world, because Lumumba said so, his mouth, his eyes, his face, his voice. She felt herself exuding beauty.[57]

Lumumba adds to Yoruba's reassurance by telling her that she would be even more beautiful with an Afro and getting a black woman singer who had worn an Afro long before it was in vogue to clip her hair. After it is over, Yoruba seems to be cut free from her need to approximate white beauty standards in order to feel pretty:

> It was just as Lumumba said it would be. Even more than he imagined. When Yoruba stared at herself in the mirror at the lady's house,...she fell angrily in love

with her reflection....She really was the Queen of Sheba....A miracle was happening. Her face aglow, a beauty from the inside bursting at the seams now, and beaming on the outside. Before her very eyes, she seemed to grow taller, as if the new person that she was becoming were too majestic for her former being. Then there was a burst of sudden revelation, and she thought, now I know the truer deeper meaning of Cotillion. Coming out! Yes! Coming out! I am a debutante coming out of my old self into a new society! She felt cotillionized for real. It was her grand debut into the maturation of her Blackness. The Rites of Cotillion had begun for her. Metamorphosis![58]

This was Yoruba's moment, a moment which had the prospect of lasting a lifetime. She was not black but comely; she was black and comely. She was coming out of colonization. She was not a debutante to high society; she was the newest ancestral link to the wondrous origin of civilization, moving closer to the black myth of identity. When Matthew saw her hair, he reveled in the woman his little girl had become, who had found the mirror of a black man's eyes to complete the act of falling in love with herself that he had begun:

Beautiful! Beautiful! A hundred million Queens of Shebas and ten million Cleopatras!...I knowed I named you right....You are truly an African beauty. Truly African beauty! So help me Brother Malcolm.[59]

And Daphne? Preparation for the cotillion also helped her to come out of colonization. Her pride was her coup de grace. Badgering Yoruba to work a white cotillion in Long Island with her as a proper prelude to the black one, she becomes an unwitting agent of her own liberation. Lumumba not only convinces Yoruba to accede to her mother's wishes, but arranges to go along himself to help demystify Daphne's idolatry of Whites. At the cotillion, he focuses on her assumption that whiteness is tantamount to civilization and her unmistakable love for Yoruba to proselyte her. From pointing out violations of etiquette at the table to violations of etiquette in the bedrooms, Lumumba made sure that Daphne swilled her fill of culture. By the time the alcohol had undressed a couple of debutantes near the bandstand, she was getting the point, and getting wearisome of it. But propriety's line of demarcation was passed when "the young gallant devils...went toward her Yoruba Evelyn, with their eyes and talk and busy hands."[60] She began to challenge "all the gay young blades with hard black looks from her cold blue eyes which had changed now to the dark consuming fires of her African mother's disposition."[61] The latent black consciousness from her remembering her mother's refusal to stay in her place as a concubine to her Scottish father — Daphne's bragging of her white ancestry, notwithstanding — comes to the fore and combines with her love for Yoruba. She had told Yoruba that she would never be a white man's concubine; now, she is certainly not going to let rich white boys violate her daughter. She admonishes Yoruba's suitors to dance with their own kind because Yoruba is a colored lady, and then begins to stand guard for Yoruba, fending off the advances of the erstwhile paragons of high society. When a fire erupts in the west wing of the mansion, her cup of white culture runs over, and she erupts: "It can't be! It can't be! It just can't be! Just can't be! They acting like niggers! Just like niggers — just like niggers."[62]

Recalling Matthew's views on white men, Daphne suspects now that he has not always been wrong, and moves hurriedly in search of Lumumba. When she finds him, she pronounces her verdict:

> Get Yoruba Evelyn and lets get out of this Godforsaken den of infidels....How can you stand any more of these white devils? Let's get out of this insane asylum, even if we have to walk all the way to the train station.[63]

Demystification. Coming out of colonization. Or almost. Lumumba had directed Daphne's eyes to the low side of white high society, and Matthew's words "cream of the crap"[64] would have been an appropriate caption for the picture that she had seen. Where now? If white did not necessarily mean pride and dignity, what about black? If the epitome of white society could act like the common low-class niggers that she had warned Yoruba about all her life, then it was left to the black elites to represent high culture. So although the white cotillion had changed Daphne, it had not worked a miracle. She is still grasping for pride and dignity; she still wants to be associated with power. Thus, when Yoruba recommends that they forget the black cotillion, Daphne suggests that they don't have to follow the example of Long Island:

> It ain't have to be like that with us Black people....We can do it differently — with dignity and elegance. It ain't have to be like these sick white peoples....It can be Black and beautiful.[65]

In that same conversation, Daphne, with her new respect for the wisdom of Matthew, admits the error of her ways, and also professes for the first time to Yoruba her love for him, branding herself a vain and foolish woman who has held on to lies because the truth did not provide enough pride and dignity. She explains her feelings for Matthew:

> I married him, because he was Black and respected me, and I thought he was beneath me and would bow down to me, his fair queen from Barbados....But through the years, I learned to love him and respect him...I know...I ain't show it all the time. But I learned his quiet pride and gentle strength....Give me credit for something, Eve-lyn. If you love both your parents,...there must have been some love in the house. I always love my family, you and Matthew, and I going always love you.[66]

The Grand Cotillion of the Femmes Fatales turned out to be life-giving. For Yoruba and Daphne, it was the culmination of their demystification of colonial cultural repression and their resistance to its dehumanization. Yoruba, in an act of further self-determination, shakily donned the African gown that Lumumba had given her to cover her body as naturally as her new coiffure was covering her head. But the Femmes Fatales failed to appreciate her new symbols, as well as the new au naturel hair styles of the other debutantes who had sworn to make the cotillion black and beautiful, and hysterically removed their wigs, trying to fit them on the renegades to conceal their black beauty. Of course, the old colonial definitions no longer fit. Of course, too, Yoruba was in double jeopardy. Lumumba intercepted her and Matthew just before they descended the stage to dance the conventional waltz, seized the mike, and urged all the Uncle Toms and Aunt Jemimas to be done with the illusions and come to the real world. Then he escorted his Queen of Sheba and her father toward the exit. Daphne screamed for them not to leave her, but was grabbed by the most staunch member of the Femmes Fatales as she left the stage. Mrs. Patterson, Chair-person of the Selection Committee for the Grand Cotillion, who had called weeks ago to inform Daphne that Yoruba had been chosen as one of five culturally deprived Harlemite girls to be a debutante and come out, now stood between her and her family. Mrs. Patterson exonerated her from the assertion of blackness, and offers her a lifetime dream:

You don't have to go...We know you didn't know about it...Stay with us, my diamond in the rough...You understand....We want you with us....Please tell me that you understand.[67]

Daphne stood there for a short lifetime, "torn between the old and new, between illusion and reality. All her life she had lived sincerely in a world of dreams and fancy." [68] Then she pulled away from Mrs. Patterson, stood more erect than she had ever stood, and made her decision: "Yes,...I understand. Finally I understand. And that's exactly why I going with my people."[69]

The Grand Cotillion had added to Daphne's demystification of colonial cultural repression. Black illusions based on white definitions were no more substantial than the white definitions were universal. So she walked away to join her family.

Two Black Poets and Responsible Power: The Power of Truth

In this final analytic chapter of specific texts, the author will treat the generative themes of mystification and dehumanization and their opposites in the poetry from 1966 to 1974 of Haki R. Madhubuti (Don L. Lee) and Sonia Sanchez. Because most of that poetry of these two black nationalist poets of the Sixties contains allusions to those themes, we shall restrict our analyses to sustained references. The general references to mystification will provide a framework for the poetic individuations of mystification and demystification. But first, let us briefly examine the black historical/artistic milieu of these poets.

Three interrelated ideas were among those that shaped that milieu: Black Power, Black Identity, and the Black Aesthetic. In 1966, Stokely Carmichael popularized the cry of Black Power on the Meredith March near Greenwood, Mississippi. Many African-Americans were becoming disenchanted with the method of non-violence and the slow progress of the Civil Rights Movement. Though some perverted the call for power into a demand to be included in this colonial system, others urged that Blacks organize around the political designation of race both to halt the physical and economic oppression that they were suffering as well as to alter this society's values. They would not be accomplices to American imperialism around the world nor to its neo-colonialism at home. This nationalism was not narrow; it pointed to Pan-Africanism, Third Worldism, and — if and when politically feasible — universal brother/sisterhood. At the same time, it recognized the necessity of appropriating the force of race that had been at the center of their exploitation.

As the author suggested in chapter one, nationalism was not new; neither was the assertion of black identity. This time, its growth was largely attributable to new internal and external factors. The black sense of self had been modified by awareness of and involvement in the civil rights and black power struggles, as well as by the rise of Africa.

The Black Aesthetic related to both power and identity. One could have neither self-determination nor self-respect if the standards that governed your art were extrinsic and effacing. The Black Aesthetic emphasized a literature of the people, by the people, and for the people. Sure, dissenters existed, but the prevailing mood was for writing that would be functional in the lives of African-Americans. The masses and the writers could contribute to each other's demystification and thus to each other's resistance to dehumanization.

Haki R. Madhubuti (Don L. Lee) and Sonia Sanchez were two poets who practiced the Black Aesthetic. They believed that all literature was necessarily political, that there was no neutral art. Thus, black writers should demystify the reality of black people and so assist in their resistance to dehumanization. As early as 1966, in the introduction to his first book, *Think Black*, Madhubuti claimed that black writers should learn from their people, give back their "knowledge to the people in a manner in which they can identify"[1] and learn, and thus become culture stabilizers. Later, Madhubuti urged the black writer to define and legitimize black reality and to "move to expose and wipe out that which is not necessary for our existence as a people."[2] As he told black poets, "if what you are to give our people is to be meaningful, it must have some relationship to reality."[3]

Sanchez also insisted that black writers aid in the process of demystifying the reality of the African-American experience. Recognizing that "this crackerized country has dealt on us and colonized us body and soul,"[4] and thus that Blacks are "the finished product of an American dream, nightmarish in concept and execution,"[5] she described the role of black writers in the journey of black people toward blackness:

> We be Word Sorcerers. Indeed. For we are the disenchanters of the gospel of inferiority, the exorcists of hatred of self, the enchanters of our renewed circle of Blackness where the love of self and each other has no Beginning or End.[6]

Madhubuti and Sanchez, then, are poets who believe that literature should aim at the metamorphosis of black people. Aware of the historical devastation of American mystification on African-Americans, they attempt to use language to invest Blacks with the power of truth against the colonizer's irresponsible power. They try, in Mari Evans' terms, to "speak the truth to the people,"[7] employing implicitly their ethos as speaker to cut through the rhetoric of the colonizer. Let us examine the poetry of Madhubuti and Sanchez from 1966 to 1974 (with the exception of Sanchez' third book, *Love Poems*, which does not deal explicitly with African-American mystification), using their general descriptions of mystification as a framework for poetic individuations of mystification and demystification.

In Madhubuti's first book, he closes the introduction with a poem that points out how the colonizer defines success for the colonized at the same time that he redirects their potential hostilities into safe channels:

America calling.
negroes.
can you dance?
play foot/baseball?
nanny?
cook?
needed now. negroes
who can entertain
ONLY.
others not
wanted.
(& are considered extremely dangerous.)[8]

The poems "The Primitive" and "The Negro (a pure product of Americanism)" in Madhubuti's second book, *Black Pride*, contain some of the strongest general references to mystification that exist in his work. In the first poem, after outlining the rape of Africa by Europeans and the attendant cultural justification that the Dark Continent needed civilizing, he turns to American methods of mystification:

christianized us.
raped our minds with:
T.V. and straight hair,
Reader's Digest and bleaching creams,
tarzan & jungle jim,
used cars & used homes,
reefers and napalm,
european history & promises.[9]

He concludes by saying that "they brought us here—/to drive us mad./ (like them)."[10] In the second poem, he emphasizes the power of the colonizer to define, whether it is black heroes or white mythological ones:

black history was booker t.
& george c. & a whi-te lie
over black truth
....
working, saving all year/
working, saving to buy
christmas gifts for children/
just to tell them a whi
te santa claus brought them.[11]

In both poems, Madhubuti decries the irresponsible power of the colonizer, the ability to make his definitions dominant using "this weapon called civilization"[12] to swing Blacks "to assimilation into whi/te madness called civilization."[13] His concern is "those alien concepts of whiteness"[14] that lead African-Americans "into aberration."[15]

In two later poems, "Blackman/an unfinished history" and "Spirit Flight into the Coming," Madhubuti summarizes the impact of mystification. In the first, after describing the black great migration dream of the melting pot, he suggests that it was Blacks who were in fact melted down:

and we burned into something different & unknown
we acquired a new ethic   a new morality   a new history
and we lost
we lost much   we lost that   that was

    we became americans   the best   the real
    and blindly accepted america's heroes as our own
    our minds wouldn't *function*.

    ....

    we took on the language, manners, mores, dress & religion
    of the people with the unusual color.
    into the 20th century we wandered rubber-stamped
    a poor copy![16]

In the second poem, Madhubuti argues that the colonizer's mystification has been so successful that many African-Americans have accepted the new forms of slavery as freedom:

    we slaves because we wanta be. we slaves because we wanta be.
    unbelievable
    but being a slave in america is *really* hip
    slaves think they can buy their freedom
    slaves drive big cars
    slaves take dope
    slaves love big houses
    slaves teach blackness at big universities
    slaves love their enemy
    slaves love death in any form
    slaves love paper money
    slaves live for pleasure only
    if we slaves be let free we'd buy ourselves back into slavery.
    it is hip being a slave in America cause we got everything
        slaves need.
    we're the richest slaves in the world.[17]

Sanchez also warns her black audience about the nature of the colonizer's mystification and its potential general effects. In her first book, *Homecoming*, she, like Madhubuti, uses direct statements antipodal to the image projected by the colonizer to assault that image. For Sanchez, the colonizer is a beast, and the most dangerous is the white liberal leader. In "the final solution," the leaders speak America as a land of freedom while continuing the slavery of Blacks. Blaming the victim for being hungry, illiterate, and criminal, they articulate their democratic plan of action for African-American problems:

> give us your
> ....
> blacks
> and we will
> let them fight
> in vietnam
> defending america's honor.
> we will make responsible
> citi/
> zens out of them or
> kill them trying.[18]

In the second book of Sanchez, *We a BaddDDD People*, there are three significant general references to colonial mystification. In "blk/chant/ (to be sed everyday / slowly)," she admonishes Blacks to repeat "we programmed fo death"[19] everyday as they reach for drugs and alcohol; perhaps then, they will begin to understand how the colonizer contains the justifiable anger of the colonized:

> each day the man/
> boy
> plans our death
> with short/bread
> for short / sighted / minds
> with junk to paralyze our
> blk/limbs from leapen on the
> wite / mutha / fucka /
> laughen at us
> from his wite / castles / of
> respectability.[20]

In "To Fanon, culture meant only one thing — an environment shaped to help us & children grow, shaped by ourselves in action against the system that enslaves us," Sanchez, after cautioning the colonized against the illusion that any of the surface manifestations of blackness can extirpate

the accumulated irresponsible power and opprobrium of the colonizer,
advises them to not be gulled by the appurtenances of liberty:

the cracker is deep
              deeper than the
400 yrs of our slavery.
we must
watch our
slavery
especially when it looks like freedom.
cuz slaves can look beautiful, talk beautifullee,
can be deceived by the DEVIL.[21]

Finally, in "a/coltrane/poem," Sanchez avers that the best black jazz
musicians, of whom John Coltrane was one, were prevented by the colonizer from commanding a decent livelihood because their music was too
political. After recommending the physical torture of all the capitalists,
especially white liberals who have defined themselves as heroes, she also
connects their lives with murder, poverty and starvation as well as the tor-
tuous mystification of the Protestant Ethic:

                       TORTURE
THEM FIRST AS THEY HAVE
                  TORTURED US WITH
PROMISES/
             PROMISES. IN WITE/AMURICA. WHEN
ALL THEY WUZ DOEN
                WAS HAVEN FUN WITH THEY
ORGIASTIC DREAMS OF BLKNESS.
                    (JUST SOME MO
CRACKERS FUCKEN OVER OUR MINDS.)[22]

In Sanchez' fourth book, *A Blues Book For Blue Black Magical Women*
(written when she was a member of Nation of Islam), she reflects their
mythology and returns ironically to her metaphor of the colonizer as a
beast. This time, however, the beast is the white devil Yacub, who has
been created by the big-headed black scientist. Thus, in this version,
Blacks are ultimately responsible for the irresponsible power of Whites,

and thus for their own mystification, because Whites are the progeny of a Black. Had Blacks stayed free of their contaminated mutations, slavery may not have followed. But according to this account of black mystification, the universe, which was black then, stopped

> to absorb this whiteness
> and we lost sight of
> our beginning
> our beginning
> to have no beginning
> means you are in the grave.[23]

For Sanchez, the major consequence of African-American mystification is their internalization of colonial values. She charges them to "push against the/devils of this world/against the creeping/witeness of they own minds."[24] More often than not, that whiteness results in black historical deracination, alienation, mutual objectification between men and women, and dependency on alcohol and other drugs.

Against this backdrop of mystification in the work of Madhubuti and Sanchez, the author will center the rest of this chapter on poetic individuations which reflect black submission to the dehumanizing forces of colonial mystification, opposition to them, or a metamorphosis from mystification to humanization.

Other than the brief anonymous individuations which reflect materialism, militarism, misidentity, Christian malleability and interracial misalliances, the poetic characterizations of both writers fasten on black celebrities in the entertainment, political or scribal worlds; relatives; and on ostensible autobiography.

Black figures in the entertainment field receive the harshest lashing for dehumanizing behavior resulting from acceptance of colonial dominant meanings. Singers are particularly berated, especially Diana Ross and the Supremes. In the early poem, "Memorial," Sanchez pronounces the Supremes dead for selling their soul by bleaching out their blackness:

> They sing rodgers
> and hart songs
> as if we didn't
> have enough andrew

sisters spitting their
whiter than mr.
clean songs in our faces.[25]

Sanchez returns to Diana and the Supremes in a later poem, "sum-
mer/time T.V./ (is witer than ever)." Again castigating the group for
"rodgers & hart/en all over the screen,"[26] she narrows her strictures to
Diana. In an intentionally ambiguous statement referring to both her wig
and her musical put-on, Sanchez accuses Diana of losing her black identity:

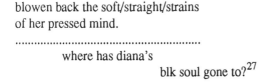

blowen back the soft/straight/strains
of her pressed mind.
....
            where has diana's
                        blk soul gone to?[27]

Madhubuti also declares the Supremes dead in his "blackmusic/a
beginning" for abandoning their musical heritage:

real sorry about
the supremes
being dead,
heard some whi
te girls
the other day—
all wigged-down
with a mean tan—
soundin just like them,
singin
rodgers & hart
& some country & western.[28]

In addition, Madhubuti singles out Diana in "On Seeing Diana go
Maddddddddd" for acceding to dehumanization at the levels of both identity and values. Informing her that some poodles in this country enjoy superior status to those Blacks who are paid by the master to walk them, as
well as that those dogs are morally superior to the masters, he reproaches

her for her shift to identification with the colonizer. He finds this especially distasteful in the wake of her own poverty:

> yr/new vision worries me because i,
> as once you, knew/know the hungry days   when
> our fathers went to ford motor co.,
> and our mothers
> in the morning traffic to the residential sections of dearborn.
> little supreme, only the well fed *forget*.[29]

Although Madhubuti suggests that he and other Blacks forgave the early disaffection, ascribing it to the mystification of success defined by the colonizer, they began to realize her internalization of that definition as she separated herself from the singing group:

> and there u stood
> a skinny earthling viewing herself as a mov
> ing star. as a mov   ing star u will travel
> north by northwest deeper into the ugliness
> of yr/bent ego.[30]

Madhubuti concludes the poem, conceding both her talent and her casualty:

> u, the gifted voice, a symphony, have now joined the
> hippy generation to become unhipped,
> to become the symbol of a new aberration,
> the wearer of other people's hair.
> to become one of the real animals of this earth.[31]

Other entertainers who reflect mystification and concomitant dehumanization are Little Anthony and the Imperials, Barbara McNair, Ray Charles and Sammy Davis, Jr. In "summer/time T.V. (is witer than ever)," Sanchez groups Little Anthony and the Imperials and Barbara Mc-Nair with Diana Ross. Her quarrel with the former is the patent attachment to this country reflected in the lyrics of one of their popular songs:

"This land
is mine.
until i
die this
land is mine."[32]

Sanchez is disturbed that "bloods be/singen bout die/en for/what ain't
even theirs/(never can be/without fighten)."[33] McNair is censured for her
desire to approximate the colonizer's standards of beauty as well as for
her preference to sing his songs:

barbara
mcnair   belts out
                    git me to the church on time
    (fo real)
                & puts her wite/soul in
to it
        and the cameraman
                            moves in for close/up
after close/up
            to show wite/
                    amu/rica
                                not all
the nigguhs want to look like
                        theyselves.
                            maybe the
country's still safe.[34]

In the previously cited "The negro (a pure product of americanism),"
Madhubuti not only disesteems Ray Charles' decision to sing "the stars
sprangle banner,"[35] but insists that "all his soul didn't change the/colors/
red, white & light blue."[36] A more extended criticism of a male enter-
tainer is provided in "See Sammy Run in the Wrong Direction (for the ten
negro editors representing n.n.p.a. who visited occupied Palestine
[known as Israel] on a fact finding trip, but upon their return — reported
few facts, if any)." Denouncing Davis' connection to Zionism and
"junior sammy davises/kissing the wailing wall/in the forgotten occupied
country."[37] Madhubuti claims that Davis' religious politics which ally

him with Israel do not allow him to be black. As a result, Davis could not even do a faithful impression of a black man:

> his inner self was   gone
> his hair turned   back
>
> ....
>
> afterall
> he was just a jewish boy
> who happened to be negro.[38]

Neither are the political and civil rights personalities Ed Brooke and Roy Wilkins authentic representations of black men in Madhubuti's poetry. In "Black Sketches," he signifies about Brooke's discomfiture at identification with black people:

> ed brooke
> sat at his
> desk
> crying & slashing
> his wrist
> because somebody
> called him
> black.[39]

In "Rise Vision Comin: May 27, 1972," written to commemorate the life of Osagyefo Kwame Nkrumah, Madhubuti advocates that Wilkins be sent to Africa to learn how to be black, since "think him have mo wisdom than the OAU/a real credit to his race."[40] Madhubuti designates him as bad credit:

> a for real beatin down negro unsure of the space he occupies
> if he occupies any him show not invisible   we see rat
>   through him
> feel his opposite a walkin back steppin X-rated movie with
> blocked vision.[41]

Sanchez brands members of her families — the one of which she is daughter and the one in which she is wife — among the dehumanized. In the wrenching "a poem for my father," she briefly but graphically traces his yielding to the colonizer's definition of black man as stud. Labeling his succumbing to that definition as makeshift manhood, she recounts all those nights with all those new women, and summarizes her response to his deformity:

> how sad it must be
> to love so many women
> to need so many black
> perfumed bodies weeping
> underneath you.[42]

Ironically, the disease of her first husband Etheridge Knight was white woe — heroin. After the "hospital/poem (for etheridge. 9/26/69)" in which she scatters the page with her viscera as she recalls the almost O.D., Sanchez settles the account in "answer to yo/question of am i not yo/woman even if you went on shit again:"

> no man.
>   blk/
>   lovers   cannot   live
> in wite powder that removes
> them from they blk/selves
>   cannot ride
>   majestic / wite / horses
>   in a machine age.
> blk / lovers
>   must live /
>   push against the
> devils of this world
>   against the creeping
> witeness of they own minds.[43]

Before we move to poetic individuations of demystification and autobiographical individuations of metamorphosis, we should briefly examine one of Madhubuti's less recognized prototypes of mystification. "Hero (a poem for brig. general frederick davison, if he can dig it)" centers on "little willie/a hero in/the american tradition./a blk/hero." A prototype for many black boys who have sought the American dream in the armed forces, little willie received the most prestigious awards for serving in arms after he is disarmed by death:

he
received his medals
p
o
s
t
h
u
m
o
u
s
l
y
.
44

In Madhubuti's poetry, two female relatives are as hopeful agents of demystification as Sanchez' father and husband figures are sad victims of mystification and dehumanization. "Big Momma," who is a member of the poet's extended family, symbolizes the practical wisdom of the black elderly who have survived. Although she expresses her identity in ways different from the young militants, Madhubuti shows that she certainly knows who she is:

she's somewhat confused about all this *blackness*
but said that's it's good when negroes start putting themselves
first and added: we've always shopped at the colored stores.[45]

Big Momma understands why drugs are so accessible in the black community. She tells the poet in his weekly ritualistic visit that the colonizer does not need to worry about a black revolution as long as he can keep drugs around:

            all he's
gotta do is drop a truck load of *dope* out
  there
on 43rd st. & all the niggers & yr
  revolutionaries
be too busy getten high & then they'll turn
  round
and fight each other over who got the
  mostest.[46]

A classical character who "never did eat too much pork/round here
anyways,"[47] this sixty-eight year old earth mother

  ...moves freely, is often right
  and when there is food
  eats joyously with her own
  real teeth.[48]

Madhubuti's real mother, though mixing whiskey with Bessie Smith to
quiet the ravages — including sexual harassment — of working in the
colonizer's kitchen to keep the poet in school, constantly reminds him
that "son you is a man, a black man"[49] in the poem "The Death Dance."
To her, homosexuals are not real men, and she shares with her son what
she observes among the colonizers:

        she talked
  about a pipe smoking sissy
  who talked sissy-talk & had
  sissy sons who were forever playing
  sissy games with themselves.[50]

One day, after dealing with the sexual pawing by her employer, she
shares an alternative perspective on the colonizer's history:

      she talked about
  the eggs of maggot colored,
  gaunt creatures from europe
  who came here/ put on pants, stopped eating with their hands

stole land, massacred indians,
hid from the sun, enslaved blacks &
thought that they were substitutes
for gods.[51]

These were not men, but the poet was a man, a black man.

The three additional poetic individuations of demystification in the poetry of Madhubuti and Sanchez are revolutionary personalties in the black world. Both poets panegyrize Malcolm X and Gwendolyn Brooks. In "Malcolm Spoke/who listened? (this poem is for my consciousness too)," Madhubuti uses Malcolm's counsel to not "wear yr/blackness in/ outer garments/& blk/slogans fr/the top 10"[52] to expose the dehumanization of black college males playing revolution. He demystifies the fervor of these young militants who wear afros and dashikis, flaunt their formal education, and fall in love with the echoes of their own pontifications while acting out the role of lover for rich white coeds. Madhubuti equates their lives with Malcolm's life before his conversion to Islam:

u are playing that
high-yellow game in blackface
minus the straighthair.

....
the double-breasted hipster
has been replaced with a
dashiki wearing rip-off.[53]

These impostors are pimping the movement.

In "Malcolm," Sanchez also employs his ideas to give voice to her sentiment that life is obscene in this colonizer's country as long as African-Americans are the footstools of Whites. Labeling Malcolm a dreamer, "the sun that tagged/the western sky and/melted tiger-scholars/while they searched for stripes,"[54] she expresses his unabashed fury at the inhumanity of the colonizer and his warning that death will no longer be reserved for the colonized:

fuck you white
man. we have been
curled too long. nothing

is sacred now. not your
white faces nor any
land that separates
until some voices
squat with spasms.[55]

As a compatriot poet, Gwendolyn Brooks receives encomium for the clarification that she brought to the work and lives of Madhubuti and Sanchez. Remembering the questions that the young self-proclaimed black revolutionary poets had about the older established writer when they first met her in the Sixties, Madhubuti retraces the path of their growing respect in "Gwendolyn Brooks:"

they listened & questioned
& went home feeling uncomfortable/unsound & so-
    untogether
they read/re-read/wrote & re-wrote
& came back the next time to tell the
lady "negro poet"
how beautiful she was/is & how she had helped them [56]

The poets saw that she wore no makeup, that her makeup was real. Madhubuti shares overheard praise:

u could hear one of the blackpoets say:
    "bro, they been callin that sister by the wrong name."[57]

In "An Afterword: for Gwen Brooks (the search for the new-song begins with the old)," he summarizes his respect for her:

to read gwen is to be,
to experience her in the *real*
is the same, she is her words,   more
like a fixed part of the world   is there
quietly penetrating   slow
....
her voice the needle for new-songs.[58]

Sanchez briefly recalls her visit with her husband Etheridge to Brooks' home in "sunday/evening at gwen's:"

saw her
naturaaal
      beauty.
           so quiet. but
full of fire
      when it bees necessary.
& we came that day
        to read our work
but left
    knooowing
      hers.[59]

In "Memorial 2. bobby hutton," Sanchez renders one meaning of the short life of the committed Black Panther:

he was denmark
vesey.
Malcolm
  garvey. all the
dead/blk/men
  of our now/time
and ago/time.[60]

She asks African-Americans to remember the long and yet growing list of audacious black men who have been destroyed by the colonizer:

check it out & don't let
it happen again.
    we got enough
blk/martyrs for all the
yrs to come.[61]

Hutton's assassination was no accident; the recurrence of such should demystify at least one phenomenon of the African-American experience:

he was
part of a long/term/plan
for blk/people.[62]

The author closes this penultimate chapter with analyses of four poems
by Madhubuti and Sanchez which appear to be autobiographical and
which show levels of metamorphical event. In "Back Again, Home (con-
fessions of an ex-executive)" and "The Only One," Madhubuti describes
his life as an executive. "The Only One," the poem reflecting the least
change, represents the one-Black-equals-integration syndrome. A faithful menial employee for fifteen years, although he had two years of college, he is now given the title executive with all the rights appertaining:
"my own desk,/(toilet, lunch area & speeches too)."[63]   Although he is
aware that his longevity is due to minding his own business and not
making any waves, the company's decision to promote him in name to a
position without description seems to increase his awareness of the
racism in the firm. It is not necessarily that he has been oblivious to his
exploitation before; rather, he sees clearly now how the colonizer can
change the form of oppression without altering the system. He is an executive because the company received pressure from civil rights forces
and needed one Black in the front office to be "an Equal Opportunity
Employer:"

They
call me an
EXECUTIVE—
but we,
you and i,

know the
Truth.[64]

In "Back Again, Home," the new black executive attempts to change
his cultural style to be successful. He dresses differently, cuts his afro,
shaves every day, and speaks the language of the colonizer when he
speaks at all. Although he is always uncomfortable, what contributes
most to the executive's demystification is the growing contradiction he
observes between his skin-deep inclusion on the job for his value to the

company and his skin-deep exclusion after five. Since he has alienated his black friends, he is alone. He resigns, and returns to his culture and community:

> out of a job—broke and hungry,
> friends are coming back—bring food,
> not quiet now—trying to speak,
> what did he say?

> "Back Again,

> BLACK AGAIN,

> Home."[65]

Sanchez has also authored two poems that indicate a personal metamorphosis. Her verse uses the institution of education rather than the work world as its focal point and gives more attention to demystification. In the title poem of her first book, *Homecoming*, she suggests that her alienation from the black community was so great after being away at college that she returned once as a tourist. However, maturity reveals the artificiality of formal training and the inadequacy of colonial accounts to explain the harsh realities of black life as well as her identity:

> now woman
> I have returned
> leaving behind me
> all those hide and
> seek faces peeling
> with freudian dreams.
> this is for real.
> black
> niggers
> my beauty.
> baby.
> i have learned it
> ain't like they say
> in the newspapers.[66]

Sanchez provides an excellent depiction of her metamorphosis to black consciousness after a college education in her extended poem, "young womanhood." Because of the length of that work and the purpose of this chapter, this author will concentrate on the tension between the reality of her book world and her growing awareness of the black world. After an unsuccessful relationship with a black man whose cynicism Sanchez does not understand, she holds on to her idealism in casual love and then enters college:

and I dressed myself
in foreign words
   became a proper painted
   european Black faced american
....
danced with white friends who
included me because that was
the nice thing to do in the late
   fifties and early sixties
and I lost myself
down roads
i had never walked.[67]

Later, as the black rebellions and the murderous colonial response to them intrude upon her idealism and integration, she is visited by visions of the murders and is taken by her gentleman friend to a white Freudian psychiatrist:

massaging his palms
he called out to me
a child of the south
and I listened to
european words
that rushed out to
me and handcuffed
me.
....

at the end of a month
when he couldn't explain
away continued acts that
killed.
at the end of a month
of stumbling alibis
after my ancestral voices
called out to me against
past and future murders,
i moved away from reconciling myself to
murderers
and gave myself up to
the temper of the times.[68]

Sanchez becomes a black activist, sings about "overcoming that which would/never come,"[69] and is knocked to the ground with her child by white policemen. The colonizers are now branded beasts, and she disgorges all the cultural repression, including "the smiles and bowings/and nods that had made/me smile so many smiles."[70] Sanchez wakes up to her blackness, alone, in "the middle sixties/full of the rising wind of history."[71] America is no longer the America of her idealism:

The repository
of european promise.
rabid america.
   Where death is
gay and obscene
and legal in the sight
of an unseeing God.[72]

Madhubuti and Sanchez continue to be poets who use the responsible power of truth to combat the colonizer's irresponsible power. In private and separate interviews which the author conducted with Sanchez and Madhubuti at Lincoln University in Pennsylvania and The Institute of Positive Education in Chicago during November, 1983, and January, 1984, respectively, each writer declared that the black poet's ultimate and inextricable responsibilities are to speak and be the truth to black people.

IX

Conclusion

Now that we have completed the analysis of the generative themes of mystification and dehumanization in the literature, their opposites, and their derivative themes, we must turn to the task of intertextualization. For it will be through some examples of intertextualizing the two autobiographies, two novels and the works of the three poets that we shall begin to see even more clearly the possibilities of realizing the three purposes of this literary criticism paradigm: to assist black students in establishing or reestablishing continuity with their culture, in understanding their cultural duality, and thus to enhance their ability to make an adequate cultural critique of the black experience.

To effect those purposes, the author will address three concerns: 1) a review of the dialectic of chronological/colonial historicity; 2) the use of Douglass' *Narrative* as a paradigmatic text in selected African-American literature; and 3) the metaphorical relationship of black students to the self-portrayals/characterizations/poetic individuations, including the intensive universality of issues that they confront with the literary generative themes, especially the archetypal pattern of cultural duality and the myths of black identity and black ethos.

By the dialectic of chronological/colonial historicity, the author means — as outlined in chapter one — the struggle, thus the tension between the passage of actual time and the stasis of colonial repression. The colonizer honors the face of the clock, but it remains in his belfry. It is he who tolls progress with empty celebrations, scattering bellwethers from the colonized to reinforce mystification. Suns are automated, and springs are grown in his greenhouse; the light and verdure bring no new dawns nor seasons for the colonized.

To convey this constancy of colonial cultural repression, the author suggests that the instructor focus on the tension in the chronological/ colonial historicity by using the recommended historical readings in the appendix or related materials in conjunction with the analyses of the literature to explore the relationship between the kaleidoscopic nature of colonial institutional forms/expressions of domination and the marginalized status of the colonized. In addition, the instructor may find the author's previously mentioned tripartite breakdown of African-American history — slavery, segregated neo-colonialism, and integrated neo-colonialism — useful for examining that tension, and for investigating what the author terms the persisting present of the African-American experience. In this study, each of those three periods is represented by two chapters.

At this juncture, we are prepared for some sampling of the intertextualizing process. The author deems that this can best be done by using Douglass' *Narrative* as the paradigmatic text. Such use will allow the literature to help make lucid both the persisting present and the intensive universality of the African-American experience. One can appropriate Douglass' antithetical terms of "irresponsible power" and "power of truth" as forces which inform mystification and demystification to apply to all the texts cited, as well as to study how they relate to the identity and ethos derivative themes of dehumanization and resistance to dehumanization, especially to the myths of black identity and black ethos. More specifically, the author contends that African-American literature suggests that the colonizer's use of "irresponsible power" to effect mystification through the institutional and informal forces of education, and through ostensible kindness aimed at the identification of the colonized with him and thus at their dehumanization. Such mystification was often attempted through the cultural hierarchies of the colonizer's status-ordering system. To resist the dehumanization at levels of identity and ethos, the colonized wielded the "power of truth" gleaned through education (formal and informal) to demystify their marginalized status. Such mystification, a customary form of the colonizer's cultural repression, is found or implied in the texts of all authors; conversely, such efforts of the colonized at demystification — the centering of their marginalized status toward the myths of black identity and black ethos, either explicit or implicit — exist in each author's work. Thus, by using Douglass' *Narrative*, written in 1845 as the paradigmatic text, we shall increase the students' ability to raise questions about the persisting present and the intensive universality of the African-American experience as we move through the literature to 1975.

The Douglass text is paradigmatic in that it contains at least seven colonial exigencies in the selected African-American literature: 1) the saturation of the derivative themes of identity and ethos; 2) the colonial attempt to mystify African-Americans through an intermixture of denial of education, colonial education and ostensible kindness: "irresponsible power;" 3) the colonial mystification objective of African-American identification with the colonizer at the levels of identity and ethos; 4) the use by the colonized of an intermixture of education — including generational wisdom of experiential communality/enclosed status community and "ebony towers" — to demystify their experience: "power of truth;" 5) the metamorphosis of the colonized toward identification with their own community at the levels of identity and ethos; 6) the mythic character of African-American self-portrayals, characterizations and poetic individuations; and 7) the intensive universality — given the first six exigencies — of those self-portrayals, characterizations and poetic individuations.

Let us examine each of these seven colonial exigencies in the Douglass *Narrative* and their parallels in the subsequent texts. Regarding the saturation of the derivative themes of identity and ethos, the author maintains that they are generic to this colonial situation, and that their depictions in these texts — with the possible exception of some of Dunbar's treatment of slave identity — reflect "a sense of fidelity to the observed and intuited truth of the Black experience." Although our discussion of the nature of cultural repression in the introduction suggested the inherency of those themes in this colonial order, the discourse on the following six specific exigencies provides concrete support for the generality.

The testimony of Douglass is probably the first unmistakably clear delineation in African-American literature of the colonizer's logic of mystification. Again, the text of Douglass' text is that the colonized must use the "power of truth" to demystify the cultural repression of the colonizer's "irresponsible power," centering their marginalized status. He foreshadows the configuration of mystification found — explicitly and implicitly — in varying degrees in the other works surveyed in this study: denial of education, colonial education and ostensible kindness. Douglass is denied education. The slavemaster Hugh Auld forbids his wife Sophia to teach Douglass to read in an effort to prevent the ascendancy of the slave's meanings. Generally, the proposed curriculum for Douglass is to learn the propriety of the slavemaster's definitions. As seen in chapter three, that included obedience, whether evoked by punishment, paltry concessions or both. Beyond learning how to say and act yes, the success of that education depended on the slave believing yes. More than once, Douglass points up the utter necessity of slave thoughtlessness for slave contentment; the slave must discern minimal inconsistencies in slavery. To promote thoughtlessness, the slavemaster not only essayed to undercut the slaves' cerebral power but also to deflect their emotive power. Douglass shows how dependency on the slavemaster was encouraged, especially through ostensible kindness. The objective of it all was slave identification with the slavemaster. Before we turn to that exigency, however, let us explore the mystification related to the other texts.

The mystification in the poems selected from Dunbar is implicit; this verse does not crystallize the colonizer's struggle to mystify the slaves. Rather, through the voice of Dunbar, the slaves speak of their mystification. Ol' Ben and the two nameless poetic individuations identify with the slavemasters to the extent that they cry and/or refuse to leave the plantations after the Civil War. And when one of the colonizers leaves the earth, the slave follows to take care of him.

In the period of segregated neo-colonialism, we discover that both Ellison's Hero and Angelou's Marguerite are besieged by mystification. The major form of mystification in Ellison's novel is the paternalism of white Marxists — who, incidentally, seem to serve as co-conspirators of black oppression. However, this segment of the text is outside the purview of this part of our analysis. Yet, we do have education and ostensible kindness at work here. In this phase of colonialism, blacks are no longer debarred from education as they were in the slave South, but the formal facet of that education is controlled by the colonizer. In the rural South of the Thirties and Forties, the setting of Ellison's novel and Angelou's autobiography, formal education for African-Americans was segregated. More important is the fact that black educators were often successfully manipulated by the colonizer to attempt to maintain his hegemony over definitions. Thus, blacks served as neo-colonial agents, perpetuating the irresponsible power of the colonizer. In return, the colonizer ceded them pseudo-power and dirty pieces of silver.

In Angelou's and Ellison's texts, we get glances at prototypes of black public school and black college administrators during that era and the mystification that the colonizer routed through them. Angelou's nameless principal, who speaks proper English and who jettisons the Negro National Anthem from the eighth grade graduation exercises because a white colonial representative is the commencement speaker, earns Marguerite's rage when that speaker, Mr. Donleavy, supports thoughtlessness by relegating all the graduates to the athletic kingdom, marching them in behind the male saints of Joe Louis and Jesse Owens. Of course, Donleavy regards his counsel, much less his appearance, as altruistic. After all, has he not put aside more important things for a few hours of imparting supreme wisdom to the lowly Negroes? Surely, such sacrifice from one situated so high in the colonial hierarchy would not fail to elicit eternal allegiance.

The colonizer only has partial success with formal education as a tool of effecting the allegiance of Marguerite. Loyalty does not follow awe if the price is her dignity. Rather, she is ready to sacrifice Donleavy to appease her gods inside that insist that she stand tall. At the same time, she measures her height in part by the yardstick of the colonizer's language: lexicon and literacy.

However, through informal education, Marguerite accepts the colonizer's standard of beauty. Those standards are both colored and colorless. In her beauty dream, she is without kink, color or cordovan eyes; yet, awake, she is conscious of her leviathan size, skinny legs, broad feet and the space between her teeth. In a time before television, in the insularity of a segregated community, the colonizer had educated Marguerite — perhaps in his cumulative culture — away from herself.

Dr. Bledsoe, president of the Negro state college, plays the role of shining ass and tinkling symbol in the mystification of hungry high school graduates. He brings Rev. Homer A. Barbees in with their soporifics, and keeps running nigger boys like the Hero, who fail to exhibit thoughtlessness to the colonizing Mr. Nortons.

Mr. Norton and the rich white men at the Battle Royal epitomize the ostensibly charitable colonizer; in fact, they work hand in hand. The white men invite the Hero to the Battle Royal to recite his high school graduation speech of humility and social responsibility. After forcing him to compete with other black boys (individualism) for counterfeit money (status) and to submit to the foreordained defeat, they allow him to repeat his oration. Then they ritualize their endorsement of his future neo-colonial leadership with a briefcase and a scholarship to the college dominated by the white philanthropist, Norton.

Killens' *The Cotillion*, depicting black life in the late Sixties, shows mystification effected through informal education — the cumulative culture of the colonizers; but as with the black school administrators in Ellison's and Angelou's work, the agent is one of the colonized, Daphne Braithwaite Lovejoy. Daphne, the mother of the protagonist, Yoruba, passes on her mystification which began in Barbados as a daughter of a white plantation owner. There, she was nonplused by the phenomenology of race and power inseparableness. This is reinforced in the United States. If white is power, white is dignity; therefore, white values are the way to dignity. In the Caribbean, she was also mystified by the acceptance of white beauty standards — especially by the Blacks in her own family — and learns to depreciate black features. In the United States, this is reinforced as well, especially by the Femmes Fatales, her black middle-class associates.

Naturally, Daphne transmits her beliefs about identity and values to Yoruba. So there is a division in Yoruba, in spite of the black perspective of her father Matthew. The conflict is greater, however, with respect to her identity. Although she probably is not as riven as Marguerite, Yoruba also doubts her beauty.

Kind whites are peripheral to the mystification in this novel, but they do exist. The impact, however, of the white Father Madison Mayfair, pastor of Daphne's Brooklyn Memorial Episcopal Cathedral, and Mr. Phil Potts, the white dance instructor for the black debutantes, is largely on Daphne.

We shall conclude our analysis of the mystification of the colonized with a brief examination of Madhubuti's and Sanchez' poetry. Although they deal with colonial education — formal and informal — and the ostensible kindness of whites as sources, their work reflects the new colonial strategies in the era of integrated neo-colonialism. Formal education now transmits the idea of integration — without black identity or values — or Black Studies with the colonizer's ethos. As in Angelou's and Ellison's work, the black heroes still have to be acceptable to the colonizer. To Joe Louis, Jesse Owens, Rev. Homer Barbee and Dr. Bledsoe have been added black successors in the integrated society, especially those projected through the mass media. Even black militants can join the canon if they reinforce colonial values. Through formal and informal education, Blacks continue to learn their place, whether in the unequal opportunity world of the workplace or within the ivory walls of the ivy towers. Ostensible white kindness is everywhere as black successes are paraded to prove that the colonizer's heart is in the right place. In addition, as poets, Madhubuti and Sanchez render mystification more patently than Dunbar, and they make general but direct statements about its impact on African-Americans as a group.

Not only is colonial mystification evident in the work of all African-American writers in this study, but also the objective of that mystification — identification with the colonizer — is a recurring motif. That identification ranges from being the property of a colonizer to believing in the propriety of his personhood and principles. Although the dominant response reflected in the self-portrayals, characterizations, and poetic individuations is resistance to this dehumanization — the centering of their marginalized status toward the myths of black identity and black ethos — there is evidence of a few slaves who scramble for status through association. They boast about their master's wealth and eclat and refuse to leave the plantation after emancipation. One slave is so distraught at the news of his master's death that he loses the will to live. In Ellison's novel, being Mr. Norton's nigger — head nigger in charge or young beneficiary — is a way to surrogate power and self. Marguerite, in Angelou's autobiography, does not identify with any one colonizer, but puts on the language of the collective elite to wear another face. Neither does Killens' Yoruba serve one colonial god; rather her desire to be a black goddess in the eyes of Lumumba is frustrated by the mystification of her mother's obsession with white beauty standards, especially with straight hair. In addition, she does have some ambivalence about the colonizer's definition of success. The roots of the famous poetic individuations of Madhubuti and Sanchez — Little Anthony, Ed Brooke, Ray Charles, Sammy Davis, Jr., Barbara McNair, Diana Ross, and Roy Wilkins — are also in the race and culture of the colonizer; they look for self in the colonizer's mirrors and manners.

However, the majority of self-portrayals, characterizations, and poetic individuations suggest demystification, identification with the black community, and thus mythic qualities. Douglass not only uses literacy's power of truth to demystify his experience and to resist the dehumanization of identification with the colonizer, but he also plies his growing

131

sense of experiential communality with the slaves — and later, free Blacks — to identify with them. Dunbar's slaves who successfully demystify their experience wield their knowledge of experiential communality to crystallize the contradictions of slavery, practice self-determination, and plan for freedom. When the Civil War comes, they put on the blue to scatter the blues. They also exercise their enclosed status community to identify with other slaves, establishing pride in their appearance, superiority of palate, and euphony. Ellison's Hero utilizes the generational wisdom of experiential communality passed on to him by his grandfather, the vet, Mary Rambo, Brother Tarp, Tod Clifton, and Ras to demystify the oppression of black people and to identify with them, recognizing the inadequacy of American democracy and Marxism in ending that oppression. Marguerite exploits the wisdom of two generations of African-American women before her — represented by her grandmother, Mrs. Flowers and her mother— to grasp the harsh physical and psychological realities of the colonized. She identifies with their misery, but not with their abjectness. Not even the most severe oppression occludes dignity. Yoruba has always related to her community; her father's black pride and activism set a persuasive example, in spite of her mother's disclaimer. Finally, not only do the poets Madhubuti and Sanchez ultimately conjoin with the black masses in their autobiographical work, but their memorable heroes such as Gwendolyn Brooks, Bobby Hutton, Big Momma, Madhubuti's mother, and Malcolm X epitomize the generational wisdom that conduces to identification with those masses.

If we examine the self-portrayals, the major characterizations, and the poetic individuations of the seven writers surveyed, the majority of them demystify their colonial realities, exhibiting racial pride and communal values, and thus exemplify the myths of black identity and black ethos. Exceptions include Dunbar's ol' Ben and the nameless poetic individuations of "The Deserted Plantation" and "The News," as well as the colonial honoraries of Madhubuti and Sanchez.

Although all of the self-portrayals and the major characterizations reflect movement toward demystification and resistance to dehumanization — except Killens' Matthew, who exhibits mythic qualities throughout the novel — Daphne's growth is the most pronounced. She exemplifies metamorphical event, as new realities — given sharper contour by Lumumba — impinge on her life, indicating that dignity is not reserved for the colonizer. In fact, she learns that the colonial objectification of black women is as rampant in the United States as in Barbados, and she will have none of that. She decides that the black bourgeoisie's unreasonable facsimile of the colonizer's culture is beneath her dignity as well. Thus, Daphne moves from mystification and dehumanization toward their opposites.

Madhubuti and Sanchez also evince metamorphical event in their autobiographical poems, but one senses that their prior mystification was not as permeative as was Daphne's. Even so, both poets show more than just a strengthening of black consciousness in that each was temporarily blinded by the colonial forces of economic mobility or formal education.

Now that we have summarized the first six colonial exigencies in the selected literature, one discerns the intensive universality of the self-portrayals, characterizations, and poetic individuations. Throughout the three historical eras of slavery, segregated neo-colonialism, and integrated neo-colonialism, all the literary figures are beset by the colonial forces of irresponsible power which attempt to deny access to the power of truth by granting status if there is identification with the colonizer's worthwhileness. For all, that proffered identification is with the colonizer's exterior, the interior of his ethos, or both. Among the colonized, there is intensive universality in the strategies of demystification at the levels of identity, values, or both. Most become (or are) examples of the myths of black identity and black ethos. And the colonized who do not secure the power of truth are clearly reduced to social death in the colonizer's world of inhumanity.

Finally, one is captured by the persisting present of colonial mystification and dehumanization as he/she proceeds through the African-American literary world from Douglass to Madhubuti and Sanchez. The irresponsible power is chameleonic but the same. As Lerone Bennett, Jr., avers:

> This system (internal colonialism), which has assumed so many forms, which has changed skin and colors and names so many times, was/is the central factor in the making of black America. Every aspect of black life and culture has been marked by it and by the struggle against it.[1]

Especially when one enfolds this literary world in that real world of Bennett's, he/she understands the dialectic of chronological/colonial historicity.

The power of truth that Bennett's understanding taps must be shared with black students. The author believes that this model of pedagogical literary criticism represents one way that the instructor can help students to gain access to that power. He submits that the expanding dream world of African-American college students, which is increasingly spun by American gods, can only be collapsed to size by assisting them in seeing the empty space. That space is both real and moral (mo real); it is not ethereal.

First, the dimensions of that dream world are an illusion. The author asserts that this model can be useful in assisting black students in discovering the intensive universality of their lives — and all the lives they know — with the literary lives. They should begin to discern the metaphorical relationship between themselves and all African-American lives. It matters not whether those other lives occupied another historical stage or whether they seem now to breathe in different and smaller worlds. As they come to grips with the cultural repression — mystification and dehumanization — of their colonial experience, they will increasingly realize that any African-American — past or present — is a metaphor for all African-Americans.

In addition, the employment of this model should help destroy another illusion of black students: that the issues they confront differ markedly from the issues of the past or the issues faced by Blacks now on the other side of their ivy walls. A literature course with this literary paradigm at its center should aid African-American students in apprehending the constancy of colonial generative themes and their derivatives, and thus to crystallize the commonality of black concerns of their time and station with the black concerns of all times and stations.

The moral space in that inflated dream world of African-American college students is soul emptiness. In stimulating black students to establish or reestablish continuity with their culture, to understand their cultural duality, and thus to make an adequate cultural critique of their historical experience, the instructor of literature can assist their re-connection to the real world, putting them in touch with the dynamic of black spirituality. It is ghastly enough that some African-Americans do not want to look like themselves or do not know how they have ever looked in the past; it is infinitely more frightening that many have adopted the same individualistic values that were responsible for the enslavement of their own people. Two black historians who are troubled by their assessment of contemporary African-American spirituality provide apt closing testimony for this study. William Strickland compares the sense of black community of the civil rights struggle years with that of now, and concludes that the spiritual degeneration is as much in black people as in the times:

> Much less of a people, much more of a heterogeneous mass. Some call this progress. I call it the americanization of the race... The destruction of that sense of community has produced this new and pernicious individualism which characterizes present-day black America.[2]

Vincent Harding, in his recent superlative history of African-Americans, *There Is A River*, caps Strickland's appraisal with an extended question which is the selfsame question of this author:

> And what now is our future, and this nation's destiny, if those costly, creative black visions of hope, long nurtured in the fires of persecution, should be broken and bastardized — or meanly forgotten — in a ruthless and unprincipled process of Americanization?[3]

APPENDIX

The Socio-Historical Context: Selected Bibliography

I. African-American General Histories by Black Historians

Allen, Robert L. *Black Awakening in Capitalist America.*
Garden City, N.Y.: Doubleday, 1970.

_____. *Reluctant Reformers: Racism and Social Reform
Movements in the United States.* Garden City, N.Y.:
Doubleday, 1975.

Bennett, Lerone, Jr. *The Shaping of Black America.*
Chicago: Johnson, 1975.

_____. *Wade in the Water.* Chicago: Johnson, 1979.

_____. *Before the Mayflower: A History of Black America.*
Chicago: Johnson, 1982.

Berry, Mary F., and John W. Blassingame. *Long Memory:
The Black Experience in America.* New York: Oxford UP, 1982.

Bontemps, Arna, and Jack Conroy. *Anyplace but Here.*
New York: Hill and Wang, 1966.

Brawley, Benjamin. *A Social History of the American Negro.*
New York: Macmillan, 1970.

Carlisle, Rodney P. *Prologue to Liberation: A History of Black
People in America.* New York: Appleton-Century-Crofts, 1972.

Coombs, Norman. *The Black Experience in America.* New York:
Twayne, 1972.

Cromwell, John W. *The Negro in American History.* Washington,
D.C.: The American Negro Academy, 1914.

Delany, Martin R. *The Condition, Elevation, Emigration and Destiny of the Colored People of the U.S..* New York: Arno, 1969.

DuBois, W.E.B. *The Gift of Black Folk: The Negroes in the Making of America.* New York: Washington Square, 1970.

Franklin, John H. *From Slavery to Freedom: A History of Negro Americans.* New York: Alred A. Knopf, 1988.

Frazier, E. Franklin. *The Negro in the United States.* New York: Macmillan, 1957.

Goode, Kenneth G. *From Africa to the U.S. and Then.* Glenview, Il.: Scott, Foresman, 1976.

Harding, Vincent. *The Other American Revolution.* Los Angeles: Center for Afro-American Studies, UCLA, 1980.

_____. *There is a River: The Black Struggle for Freedom in America.* New York: Harcourt Brace Jovanovich, 1981.

Hercules, Frank. *American Society and Black Revolution.* New York: Harcourt Brace Jovanovich, 1972.

Hodges, Norman E.W. *Black History.* New York: Monarch, 1971.

_____. *Breaking the Chains of Bondage: Black History from its Origins in Africa to the Present.* New York: Simon and Schuster, 1972.

Lincoln, C. Eric. *The Negro Pilgrimage in America.* New York: Bantam, 1967.

Logan, Rayford W. *The Negro in the United States.* Princeton, N.J.: Van Nostrand, 1957.

_____, and Irvin S. Cohen. *The American Negro*. Boston: Houghton Mifflin, 1967.

McQuilkin, Frank. *Think Black*. New York: Bruce, 1970.

Peeks, Edward. *The Long Struggle for Black Power*. New York: Charles Scribner's Sons, 1971.

Pennington, James W.C. *A Textbook of the Origin and History of the Colored People*. Detroit: Negro History, 1969.

Quarles, Benjamin. *The Negro in the Making of America*. New York: Collier, 1987.

Redding, Saunders. *The Lonesome Road: A Narrative History of Blacks in America*. Garden City, N.Y.: Doubleday, 1973.

_____.*They Came in Chains: Americans from Africa*. New York: J.B. Lippincott, 1973.

Sinclair, William A. *The Aftermath of Slavery*. New York: Arno, 1969.

Toppin, Edgar A. *Blacks in America: Then and Now*. Boston: Christian Science, 1969.

Washington, Booker T. *A New Negro for a New Century*. Miami: Mnemosyne, 1969.

Williams, George W., and Charles H. Wesley. *A History of the Negro Race in America from 1619 to 1880*. New York: Putnam and Sons, 1883.

Woodson, Carter G. *The Negro in Our History*. Washington, D.C.: The Associated Publishers, 1972.

II. Slavery: General Studies of Slave Community

A. Books

1. Blassingame, John W. *The Slave Community.* 2nd ed.
    New York: Oxford UP, 1979.

2. Genovese, Eugene. *Roll, Jordan, Roll.* New York: Pantheon,
    1974.

3. Gilmore, Al-Tony, ed. *Revisiting Blassingame's THE SLAVE
    COMMUNITY: The Scholars Respond.* Westport, Ct.:
    Greenwood, 1978.

4. Gutman, Herbert G. *The Black Family in Slavery and Freedom,
    1750-1925.* New York: Random House, 1976.

5. Huggins, Nathan I. *Black Odyssey: The Afro-American Ordeal
    in Slavery.* New York: Random House, 1979.

6. Levine, Lawrence, W. *Black Culture and Black Consciousness.*
    New York: Oxford UP, 1977.

7. Miller, Randall M. *The Afro-American Slaves: Community or
    Chaos?* Malabar, Fl.: Krieger, 1981.

8. Owens, Leslie H. *This Species of Property: Slave Life and
    Culture in the Old South.* New York: Oxford UP, 1976.

9. Rawick, George P. *From Sundown to Sunup: The Making of
    the Black Community.* Westport, Ct.: Greenwood, 1972.

10. White, Deborah, G. *Aren't I A Woman: Female Slaves in the
    Plantation South.* New York: W.W. Norton, 1985.

B. Articles

1. Berlin, Ira. "Time, Space, and the Evolution of Afro-American
    Society on British Mainland North America." *American
    Historical Review*. 85 (1980): 44-78.

2. Clarke, John H. "African Cultural Continuity and Slave Revolts
    in the New World," Parts 1 and 2. *Black Scholar*. 8.1-2
    (1976): 41-49, 2-9.

3. Davis, Angela. "Reflections on the Black Woman's Role in the
    Community of Slaves." *Black Scholar*. 3.4 (1971): 2-15.

4. Franklin, Vincent P. "Slavery Personality, and Black Culture —
    Some Theoretical Issues." *Phylon*. 35 (1974): 54-63.

5. Kolchin, Peter. "Reevaluating the Antebellum Slave Community:
    A Comparative Perspective." *Journal of American
    History*. 70 (1983): 579-601.

III. Segregated Neo-Colonialism, 1877-1954: General Studies

A. Books

1. Bracey, John et al. *The Rise of the Ghetto*. Belmont, Ca.:
    Wadsworth, 1971

2. Bunche, Ralph H. *The Political Status of the Negro in the Age
    of FDR*. Chicago: U. of Chicago Pr., 1973.

3. Kifer, Allen. *The Negro Under the New Deal, 1933-1941*.
    Diss., U. of Wisconsin, 1961.

4. Kirby, John B. *Black Americans in the Roosevelt Era*. Knoxville,
    Te.: U. of Tennessee Pr., 1980.

5. Logan, Rayford. *The Betrayal of the Negro: From Rutherford B. Hayes to Woodrow Wilson*. New York: Macmillan, 1965.

6. Sitkoff, Harvard. *A New Deal for Blacks*. New York: Oxford UP, 1981.

7. Sochen, June. *The Unbridgeable Gap: Blacks and Their Quest for the American Dream, 1900-1930*. Chicago: Rand McNally, 1972.

8. _____, ed. *The Black Man and the American Dream: Negro Aspirations in America, 1900-1930*. Chicago: Quadrangle, 1971.

9. Sternsher, Bernard, ed. *The Negro in Depression and War: Prelude to Revolution, 1930-1945*. Chicago: Quadrangle, 1969.

10. Wolters, Raymond. *Negroes and the Great Depression*. Westport, Ct.: Greenwood, 1970.

B. Articles

1. Dalifume, Richard M. "The 'Forgotten Years' of the Negro Revolution." *Journal of American History*. 55 (1968): 90-106.

2. DuBois, W.E.B. "Race Relations in the United States, 1917-1947." *Phylon*. 9 (1948): 236-41.

3. Fishel, Leslie H. Jr. "The Negro in the New Deal Era." *Wisconsin Magazine of History*. 48 (1964): 111-26.

4. Sears, James M. "Black Americans and the New Deal." *The History Teacher*. 10 (1976): 89-105.

5. Wye, Christopher G. "The New Deal and the Negro Community."
    Journal of American History. 59 (1972): 621-39.

IV. Integrated Neo-Colonialism, 1954-Present: General Studies

A. Books

1. Bracey, John et al. *Conflict and Competition: Studies in the
    Recent Black Protest Movement.* Belmont, Ca.:
    Wadsworth, 1971.

2. Blair, Thomas L. *Retreat to the Ghetto: The End of a Dream?*
    New York: Hill and Wang, 1977.

3. Blumberg, Rhoda L. *Civil Rights: The Nineteen Sixties Freedom
    Struggle.* Boston: Twayne, 1984.

4. Brisbane, Robert H. *Black Activism: Racial Revolution in the
    United States, 1954-1970.* Valley Forge, Pa.: Judson, 1974.

5. Carson, Clayborne. *In Struggle: SNCC and the Black Awakening
    of the 1960s.* Cambridge: Harvard UP, 1981.

6. Levitan, Sar A. et al. *Still A Dream: The Changing Status of
    Blacks Since 1960.* Cambridge: Harvard UP, 1975.

7. Marable, Manning. *Race, Reform and Rebellion: The Second
    Reconstruction in Black America, 1945-1982.* Jackson:
    UP of Mississippi, 1984.

8. Meier, August and Elliott Rudwick, eds. *Black Protest in the
    Sixties.* Chicago: Quadrangle, 1970.

9. Morris, Aldon D. *The Origins of the Civil Rights Movement:
    Black Community Organizing for Change.* New York:
    Free, 1984.

10. Sitkoff, Harvard. *The Struggle for Black Equality, 1954-1980*. New York: Warner, 1980.

B. Articles

1. Blassingame, John. "The Revolution That Never Was: The Civil Rights Movement, 1950-1980." *Perspectives*. (Summer 1982): 3-15.

2. Harding, Vincent. "The Black Wedge in America: Struggle, Crisis and Hope, 1955-1975." *Black Scholar*. 7.4 (1975): 28-46.

3. Karenga, Maulana. "From Civil Rights to Human Rights: Social Struggles in the Sixties." *Black Collegian*. (Feb.-Mar. 1980): 122-27.

4. Sizemore, Barbara. "Sexism and the Black Male." *Black Scholar*. 4.6-7 (1973): 2-11.

5. Strickland, William. "The Road Since Brown: The Americanization of the Race." *Black Scholar*. 11.1 (1979): 2-8.

V. **Analyses Reflecting Dialectic of Chronological/Colonial Historicity**

A. Books

1. Ballard, Allen B. *The Education of Black Folk*. New York: Harper & Row, 1973.

2. Berry, Mary F., and John W. Blassingame. *Long Memory: The Black Experience in America*. New York: Oxford UP, 1982.

3. Blauner, Robert. *Racial Oppression in America.* New York: Harper & Row, 1972.

4. Franklin, John H. *Racial Equality in America.* Chicago: U. of Chicago Pr., 1976.

5. Gerster, Patrick, and Nicholas Cords. *Myth in American History.* Encino, Ca.: Glencoe, 1977.

6. Gregory, Dick. *No More Lies: The Myth and the Reality of American History.* New York: Harper & Row, 1971.

7. Knowles, Louis L. and Kenneth Prewitt, eds. *Institutional Racism in America.* Englewood Cliffs, N.J.: Prentice-Hall, 1969.

8. Lacy, Dan. *The White Use of Blacks in America.* New York: McGraw-Hill, 1972.

9. Ringer, Benjamin B. *'We The People' and Others: Duality and America's Treatment of its Racial Minorities.* New York: Tavistock, 1983.

10. Turner, Jonathan H., Royce Singleton, Jr., and David Musick. *Oppression: A Socio-History of Black-White Relations in America.* Chicago: Nelson-Hall, 1984.

B. Articles

1. Allen, Robert. "A Historical Synthesis: Black Liberation and World Revolution." *Black Scholar.* 4.6 (1972): 7-23.

2. Bennett, Lerone, Jr. "The System." *The Shaping of Black America.* Lerone Bennett, Jr. Chicago: Johnson, 1975.

3. Feagin, Joe. "Slavery Unwilling to Die: The Background of Black Oppression in the 1980s." *Journal of Black Studies.* 17 (1986): 173-200.

4. O'Dell, J.H. "Colonialism and the Negro American Experience," Parts 1 and 2. *Freedomways.* 6.3-4 (1966): 296-308, 7-15.

5. Staples, Robert. "Race and Colonialism." *Black Scholar.* 7.9 (1976): 37-49.

147

Notes

Introduction

1
Muhammad Ahmed, "On the Black Student Movement, 1960-1970," *Black Scholar* 12.5 (1980); S.E. Anderson, "Black Students: Racial Consciouness and the Class Struggle, 1960-1976," *Black Scholar* 8. 3 (1977); K. Sue Jewell, "Will the Real Black, Afro-American, Mixed, Colored, Negro Please Stand Up?" *Journal of Black Studies* 16. 1 (1985); Joseph McCormick, "Survey of Black Middle Class Students," *The Hilltop* 70. 23 (1987); Ronald Walters, "The Black Education Strategy in the 1970's," *The Journal of Negro Education* 48. 2 (1979). Luke Tripp, Black Student Activists. (Lanham, Md.: University Pr. of America, 1987.)

2
Houston A. Baker, Jr. *Long Black Song: Essays in Black American Literature and Culture* (Charlottesville: U. Pr. of Virginia, 1972) 1.

3
Jane Campbell, *Mythic Black Fiction: The Transformation of History* (Knoxville: U. of Tennessee Pr., 1986) X.

4
Jay Wright, "Desire's Design, Vision's Resonance," *Callaloo* 10. 1 (1987): 14.

5
Wright 14.

6
Paulo Freire, *Pedagogy of the Oppressed* (New York: Seabury, 1974) 91.

7

Freire 93.

8

Orlando Patterson, *Slavery and Social Death* (Cambridge: Harvard UP, 1982) 5.

9

Harold Cruse, *Rebellion or Revolution?* (New York: William Morrow, 1969) 77.

10

Houston A. Baker, Jr., "On the Criticism of Black American Literature: One View of the Black Aesthetic," in *Reading Black: Essays in the Criticism of African, Caribbean, and Black American Literature*, ed. Houston A. Baker, Jr. Ithaca: Cornell University Africana Studies and Research Center, 1976) 56.

11

Norman Harris, "The Black Universe in Contemporary Afro-American Fiction," *CLA Journal* 30. 1 (1986): 1.

12

The author believes that not only must internal colonialism be accepted as an appropriate designation for the African-American experience, but that it also must be admitted that the experience has been one which he labels consummate colonialism. By that, he means a configuration of certain historical forces has produced a system of cultural repression without peer in the annals of colonialism. This cultural repression — one of five constants of all colonialism, including economic exploitation, political control, racism, and force, according to Bennett — seems intertwined at once with the other four constants and the following historical forces:

1) Slavery. The nature of the initial/early contact with the
colonizer is not only significant in this study because of
the horrors inherent in slavery, but also because of the
racist ideology that underpinned the economic exploitation.

The colonizer's attempt at what Cesaire called "thingifica-
tion" was an effort to erase the humanity (dehumanization)
of the captive by institutionalizing (mystifying) the captor's
norms of identity and values as universal. Where that institutionalization succeeded with the colonized, it required disassociation from Africa, her blackness and way of life. Where
it succeeded with the colonizer or the colonized, it reinforced
a status-ordering system based upon the notion that "white is
right."

2) Time of "overlordship." Bennett uses this term in arguing
that the African-American's longer period of white overlordship made it no less a colonial situation. Rather, this author
suggests that it has contributed to an intensification of cultural
repression.

3) Space. Although large plantation life and subsequent segregated rural and urban life engendered conditions that strengthened communalism and thus colonized resistance to cultural
repression, the more direct and sustained contact of the colonized with the colonizer and his way of life — individualism/
materialism — on the small slave farms and in subsequent
"integrated" experiences increased the possibilities that the resistance would not develop as much. Now in addition, the cap-
italistic-controlled mass media have reduced that positive impact of physical segregation. Pinkney submits that the greater
direct contact of the colonized with the colonizer in an internal
colonial circumstance may lead "to greater psychic damage in
the form of self-hatred which leads to confused identities."
Certainly, it may also affect values.

4) Being a minority. Especially in integrated milieus, this may
create greater anxiety for the colonized who have not demystified their history. Sylvia Hill explains that Cabral believed
that the minority status of Africans in the diaspora "has had
its impact on their concept of the focus of struggle." He thought
that their "marginal status in a 'racist or colonial metropolis'
...formed the material basis that gave rise to the need for cul-

tural identity in the form of Pan-Africanism or the Negritude Movement." Bennett suggests that another consequence of blacks being a minority in this country is a sense of impotence "in the midst of a hostile and/or indifferent white population with overwhelming numerical and strategic superiority."

5) Overwhelming power of whites. Only a few times during their colonial experience have African-Americans organized or threatened to organize against representatives of the State. Only in a few slave insurrections on large plantations and in a few small displays of self-defense in rudimentary plans for urban guerilla war in the late Sixties by such organizations as the Black Panthers and the Revolutionary Action Movement (RAM), have blacks organized to challenge the awesome power associated with whites. In sum, there has been negligible romanticizing about physically opposing what has become the most powerful nation on the globe. Further, even most one-on-one confrontations of whites and blacks have been conditioned by the many reminders of this imbalance of numbers and access to force.

6) The land issue. Whites did not settle on the homeland of African-Americans, nor were blacks victimized there. The result has been less black identification with land than in classical colonialism, although Southern rural blacks have historically developed a significant attachment to the land of their roots.

7) The language issue. African-Americans have no native language, although they have a hybrid one which distinguishes them from the colonizer. Consequently, blacks have been forced to conceptualize and communicate in the colonizer's language, with the attendant dangers of cultural repression.

8) The religion issue. African-Americans do not have a native religion, although they possess different hybrid ones. Further, denominational and ideological differences have under-

mined the role which the church — the sole institution which blacks control — could have assumed in resisting colonialism. The author must hastily add that the African-American church, invisible and formally organized, has acted at certain critical times — for instance, during slavery and the civil rights movement — as a positive force in combating colonialism.

9) The education issue. Although, as Memmi points out, all schools in a colonial situation are designed to effect cultural repression and thus to promote a permanent duality in the colonized, the prospects of that purpose being achieved were heightened in this country by altered circumstances in the present period of integrated neo-colonialism. In particular, the increased direct contact of young black intellectuals with the colonizers and their individualistic/materialistic ethos in integrated educational institutions, the illusions of progress in the outlawing of segregated institutions, and the actual economic advancement of swelling numbers of blacks in attendance at college contributed to what Strickland calls "the Americanization of the race."

10) Material advantages for the colonized. It is generally accepted that not only are African-Americans richer as a group than any other colonized group in the world, but that also there are larger proportions of the petite bourgeoisie among African-Americans than among any other colonized group. As Staples affirms, "the colonized minorities in the United States...have greater material advantages than their international counterparts." S.E. Anderson, African-American activist scholar, uncovers some very disconcerting implications of blacks' position as the most "privileged" of the colonized. He declares that blacks are "aiding and benefitting from White America's global exploitation...and (that) by demanding more jobs, higher wages, better welfare, medical care, education, housing, etc., we are simultaneously maintaining our 'privileged' colonized status and helping the third world become even more under-developed." In fact, the material

disparity between African-Americans and the third world continues to widen.

13

Isadore Okpewho as quoted in Wright, 27.

14

Nancy Arnez as quoted in Carol F. Elder, "The Discovery of America: Literary Nationalism in the Criticism of Black American Literature," diss., U. of Pittsburgh, 1982, 166.

15

Eugenia W. Collier, "Steps Toward a Black Aesthetic: A Study of Black American Literary Criticism," diss., U. of Maryland, 1976, 1.

16

Mari Evans, "Decolonialization as Goal: Political Writing as Device," *First World* 2. 3 (1979): 37.

17

Evans 37.

18

Mari Evans, "A Critical Approach to Black Literature: The Classroom Connection," UCLA Center for Afro-American Studies Spring Symposium, Los Angeles, 23 April, 1983, 30.

Chapter 1

1

Amilcar Cabral, *Return to the Source* (New York: Africa Information Service, 1973) 62.

2

Frantz Fanon, *The Wretched of the Earth* (New York: Grove, 1969) 208.

3
Albert Memmi, *The Colonizer and the Colonized* (Boston: Beacon, 1967) XII.

4
Cabral 39, 43.

5
Albert Memmi, *Dominated Man* (Boston: Beacon, 1968) 193.

6
Memmi, *Dominated* 197.

7
Cabral 40.

8
Memmi, *Colonizer* XII.

9
Memmi, *Dominated* 23.

10
Fanon, *Wretched* 211.

11
Memmi, *Colonizer* 11.

12
Memmi, *Dominated* 23.

13
Fanon, *Wretched* 210, 236.

14
Memmi, *Colonizer* 105, 106.

15
Sylvia Hill, "International Solidarity: Cabral's Legacy to the African-American Community," *Latin American Perspectives* 11. 2 (1984): 76.

16
Hill 76.

17
Memmi, *Colonizer* 91.

18
Memmi, *Colonizer* 92.

19
Memmi, *Colonizer* 103.

20
Cabral 66.

21
Cabral 59.

22
Cabral 53.

23
Fanon, *Wretched* 216.

24
Fanon, *Wretched* 233.

25
Cabral 48.

26
Memmi, *Dominated* 27-8.

27
Memmi, *Dominated* 28.

28
Fanon, *Wretched* 247.

29
Fanon, *Wretched* 247-8.

30
J.H. O'Dell, "A Special Variety of Colonialism," *Freedomways* 7 (1967): 8.

31
Rodney Carlisle, *The Roots of Black Nationalism* (Port Washington, N.Y.: Kennikat Pr., 1975) 4.

32
Alphonso Pinkney, *Red, Black, and Green: Black Nationalism in the United States* (Cambridge: Cambridge UP, 1976) 3.

33
Arthur L. Mathis, "Social and Psychological Characteristics of the Black Liberation Movement: A Colonial Analogy," diss., U. of Michigan, 1971, 43.

34
John H. Bracey, Jr., "Black Nationalism Since Garvey," *Key Issues in the Afro-American Experience* 2 vols., ed. Nathan Huggins et al (New York: Harcourt Brace, 1971) vol. 2, 259.

35
Lerone Bennett, Jr., *The Shaping of Black America* (Chicago: Johnson, 1975) 208.

36
Robert Blauner, *Racial Oppression in America* (New York: Harper & Row, 1972) 83, 84.

37

J.H. Howard, "Toward a Social Psychology of Colonialism," *Black Psychology*, ed. Reginald L. Jones (New York: Harper & Row, 1980) 370.

38
Bennett 218.

39

J.H. O'Dell, "Colonialism and the Negro American Experience," *Freedomways* 6 (1966): 300.

40
O'Dell, "Colonialism" 301.

41
O'Dell, "Colonialism" 305.

42
O'Dell, "Colonialism" 308.

43

Robert Staples, "Race and Colonialism: The Domestic Case in Theory and Practice," *Black Scholar* 7. 9 (1976): 41.

44
Bennett 218-19.

45
Bennett 220.

46
Bennett 220.

47

William Strickland, "The Road Since Brown: The Americanization of the Race," *Black Scholar* 11. 1 (1979): 6.

48
Richard Wright as quoted in Ellen Wright and Michel Fabre's *Richard Wright Reader* (New York: Harper & Row, 1978) XVII.

49
Wright and Fabre XVII.

50
Bennett 208.

51
O'Dell, "Special Variety of Colonialism" 8.

52
James Turner, "Black America: Colonial Economy Under Siege," *First World* 1. 2 (1977): 9.

53
Staples 44.

54
Staples 43.

55
Staples 43.

56
Staples 40.

57
Herman George, Jr., *American Race Relations Theory* (Lanham, Md.: University Pr. of America, 1984) 87.

58
Blauner 91.

59
Blauner 84.

60
Staples 39.

61
Molefi Asante, Paper, 1985 National Council for Black Studies Conference, Ithaca, N.Y., 29 Mar. 1985.

62
Staples 39.

63
Staples 40.

64
Harold Cruse, "The Creating and Performing Arts and the Struggle for Identity and Credibility," *Negotiating the Mainstream: A Survey of the Afro-American Experience*, ed. Harry A. Johnson (Chicago: ALA, 1978) 102.

65
Jomills H. Braddock, "Internal Colonialism and Black American Education," *Western Journal of Black Studies* 2. 1 (1978): 32.

66
Patti M. Peterson, "Colonialism and Education: The Case of the Afro-American," *Comparative Education Review* (June 1971): 146.

67
Bennett 211.

68
Bennett 211.

69
Douglas Davidson, "The Furious Passage of the Black Graduate Student," *The Death of White Sociology,* ed. Joyce A. Ladner (New York: Random House, 1973) 31-2.

70

Houston A. Baker, Jr., *The Journey Back: Issues in Black Literature and Criticism* (Chicago: U. of Chicago Pr., 1980) 130.

71

Baker, *Journey Back* 130.

72

James Turner and W. Eric Perkins, "Towards a Critique of Social Science," *Black Scholar* 7. 7 (1976): 8.

73

Braddock 32.

74

James Turner, "Black Nationalism," *Topics in Afro-American Studies*, ed. Henry J. Richards (Buffalo: Black Academy, 1971) 70.

75

Turner, "Black Nationalism" 70.

76

Turner and Perkins, "Towards a Critique" 8.

77

Turner and Perkins, "Towards a Critique" 7.

78

Turner and Perkins, "Towards a Critique" 7.

79

Baker, *Journey Back* 130.

80

Turner and Perkins, "Towards a Critique" 10.

81
Louis B. Williams and Mohamed El-Khawas, "A Philosophy of Black Education," *Journal of Negro Education* 47 (1978): 181.

82
Mathis 121.

83
Turner, "Black Nationalism" 72-3.

84
Turner, "Black Nationalism" 73.

Chapter 2

1
Frantz Fanon, *The Wretched of the Earth* (New York: Grove, 1968) 222.

2
Frantz Fanon, *Black Skin, White Masks* (New York: Grove, 1967) 184.

3
Amilcar Cabral, *Return to the Source* (New York: Africa Information Service, 1973) 68.

4
Cabral 68.

5
Albert Memmi, *The Colonizer and the Colonized* (Boston: Beacon, 1967) 110.

6
Fanon, *Wretched* 225.

7
Fanon, *Wretched* 225.

8
Fanon, *Wretched* 225.

9
Fanon, *Wretched* 225, 232.

10

Fanon, *Wretched* 227.

11
Fanon, *Wretched* 231.

12
Fanon, *Wretched* 231.

13
Fanon, *Wretched* 231.

14
Fanon, *Wretched* 231.

15
Fanon, *Black Skin* 184.

16
Keneth Kinnamon, "The Political Dimension of Afro-American Literature," *Soundings* 4. (1977): 131.

17
David F. Dorsey, "The Dual Aesthetic of Black American Artists," *Beyond Black or White: An Alternate America*, eds. Vernon J. Dixon and Badi Foster (Boston: Little, Brown, 1971) 78.

18
Donald B. Gibson, "Individualism and Community in Black American History and Fiction," *Black American Literature* 11. (1977): 124.

19
Kinnamon 144.

20
Eugenia Collier, "Steps Toward a Black Aesthetic: A Study of Black American Literary Criticism," diss., U. of Maryland, 1976, 190, 137.

21
Collier 135.

22
Richard Wright, "Blueprint for Negro Writing," *Richard Wright Reader*, eds. Ellen Wright and Michel Fabre (New York: Harper & Row, 1978) 42.

23
Wright 48.

24
Wright 43.

25
Wright 45

26
Wright 46.

27
Wright 47.

28
Kinnamon 144.

29

Ron Karenga, "Black Cultural Nationalism," *The Black Aesthetic*, ed. Addison Gayle, Jr. (Garden City, N.Y.: Doubleday, 1971) 35,34, 37.

30

Addison Gayle, Jr., "Blueprint for Black Criticism," *First World* 1. 1 (1977): 44.

31

Albert Memmi, *The Colonizer and the Colonized* (Boston: Beacon, 1967) 91.

32

Gayle 43.

33

Carol F. Elder, "The Discovery of America: Literary Nationalism in the Criticism of Black American Literature," diss., U. of Pittsburgh, 1982, 183.

34

Elder 183.

35

Carolyn F. Gerald, *Black Arts and Black Aesthetics* (Atlanta: First World, 1981) XIV.

36

Donald B. Gibson, *The Politics of Literary Expression* (Westport, Ct.: Greenwood, 1981) 7.

37

Jerry W. Ward, Jr., "The Black Critic as Reader," *Black American Literature Forum* 14. 1 (1980): 23.

38

Ward, "Black Critic" 23.

39

Mari Evans, "Decolonization as Goal: Political Writing as Device," *First World* 2. 3 (1979): 34.

40

Evans, "Decolonization" 34.

41

Mari Evans, "A Critical Approach to Black Literature: The Classroom Connection," UCLA Center for Afro-American Studies Spring Symposium, Los Angeles, 23 April, 1983, 19.

42

Evans, "Critical Approach" 20.

43

Evans, "Critical Approach" 1.

44

Evans, "Critical Approach" 16.

45

Jerry W. Ward, Jr., "A Black and Crucial Enterprise: An Interview with Houston A. Baker, Jr." *Black American Literature Forum* 16.2 (1982): 52

46

Ward, "Black and Crucial Enterprise" 51.

47

Stephen Henderson, *Understanding the New Black Poetry: Black Speech and Black Music as Poetic References* (New York: William Morrow, 1973) 62.

48

Paulo Freire, *Pedagogy of the Oppressed* (New York: Seabury, 1974) 91-2.

49
Freire 93.

50
Freire 93.

Chapter 3

1
Frederick Douglass, *Narrative of the Life of Frederick Douglass, an American Slave*, ed. Houston A. Baker, Jr. (New York: Penguin, 1982) 84, 77.

2
Douglass 78.

3
Douglass 78.

4
Douglass 78.

5
Douglass 78.

6
Douglass 84.

7
Douglass 82.

8
Douglass 139-40.

9
Douglass 105.

10
 Douglass 84.

11
Douglass 135.

12
Douglass 56.

13
Douglass 116.

14
Douglass 115.

15
Douglass 115.

16
Douglass 115-16.

17
Douglass 116.

18
Douglass 62-63.

19
Douglass 63.

20
Douglass 63.

21
Douglass 63.

22
Douglass 56, 54.

23
Douglass 56.

24
Douglass 56.

25
Douglass 57.

26
Douglass 58.

27
Douglass 53.

28
Douglass 98.

29
Douglass 98.

30
Douglass 74.

31
Douglass 77.

32
Douglass 90.

33
Douglass 117.

34
Douglass 117.

35
Douglass 121.

36
Douglass 82.

37
Douglass 97.

38
Frantz Fanon, *The Wretched of the Earth* (New York: Grove, 1968) 94.

39
Douglass 111.

40
Douglass 112.

41
Douglass 113.

42
Douglass 113.

43
Douglass 141.

44
Douglass 54.

45
Douglass 90.

46
Douglass 143.

47
Douglass 143.

48
Douglass 137.

49
Douglass 138.

50
Douglass 138.

51
Douglass 138.

52
Douglass 120.

53
Douglass 120, 121.

54
Douglass 121.

55
Douglass 122.

56
Douglass 129-30.

57
Douglass 121-22.

58
Douglass 151.

59
Douglass 151.

60
Douglass 151.

61
Douglass 159.

62
Douglass 159.

63
Douglass 149.

Chapter 4

1
Paul L. Dunbar, *The Complete Poems of Paul Laurence Dunbar* (New York: Dodd, Mead, 1962) VIII-IX.

2
Dunbar IX-X.

3
Houston A. Baker, Jr., *Singers of Daybreak* (Washington, D.C.: Howard UP 1974) 33-41.

4
Bruce D. Dickson, Jr., "On Dunbar's 'Jingles in a Broken Tongue.'" *A Singer in the Dawn*, ed. Jay Martin (New York: Dodd, Mead, 1975) 94-113.

5
James A. Emanuel, "Racial Fire in the Poetry of Paul Laurence Dunbar," *A Singer in the Dawn*, ed. Jay Martin (New York: Dodd, Mead, 1975) 75-93.

6
Gossie H. Hudson, "Paul Laurence Dunbar: Dialect et la Negritude," *Phylon* 34. 3 (1973): 236-47.

7
Darwin T. Turner, "Paul Laurence Dunbar: The Rejected Symbol," *Journal of Negro History* 52 (1967): 1-13. Also "Paul Laurence Dunbar: The Poet and the Myths" *Phylon* 43 (1974): 155-171.

8
Jay Martin, ed. *A Singer in the Dawn* (New York: Dodd, Mead, 1975) 13.

9
Dunbar 201.

10
Dunbar, 475.

11
Benjamin Brawley, *Paul Laurence Dunbar* (Chapel Hill: North Carolina UP 1936) 73.

12
Jay Martin and Gossie H. Hudson, eds., *The Paul Laurence Dunbar Reader* (New York: Dodd, Mead, 1975) 262.

13
Hudson, "Paul Laurence Dunbar" 240.

14
Dunbar 107-108.

15
Dunbar 218.

16
Dunbar 219-20.

17
Dunbar 32.

18
Dunbar 234.

19
Dunbar 340-41.

20
Dunbar 302.

21
Dunbar 313-14.

22
Dunbar 417-18.

23
Dunbar 215.

24
Dunbar 316-17.

25
Dunbar 334.

26
Dunbar 429.

27
Dunbar 219.

28
Dunbar 229.

29
Dunbar 246.

30
Dunbar 270.

31
Dunbar 302-03.

32
Dunbar 325.

33
Dunbar 20.

34
Dunbar 20-21.

35
Dunbar 21.

36
Dunbar 22.

37
Dunbar 22.

38
Dunbar 22-23.

39
Dunbar 7.

40
Dunbar 32.

41
Dunbar 234.

42
Dunbar 243.

43
Dunbar 235.

44
Dunbar 234.

45
Dunbar 234.

46
Dunbar 240-41.

47
Dunbar 385.

48
Dunbar 253.

49
Dunbar 293-94.

50
Dunbar 294.

51
Dunbar 294-45.

52
Dunbar 295.

53
Dunbar 316.

54
Dunbar 313.

55
Dunbar 346.

56
Dunbar 214-15.

57
Dunbar 418.

58
Dunbar 279.

59
Dunbar 239-40.

60
Dunbar 131.

61
Dunbar 286.

62
Dunbar 287.

63
Dunbar 226-27.

64
Dunbar 247.

65
Dunbar 303.

66
Dunbar 430.

Chapter 5

1
Ralph Ellison, *Invisible Man* (New York: Signet, 1952) 499.

Chapter 6

1
Maya Angelou, *I Know Why the Caged Bird Sings* (New York: Bantam, 1971) 3.

2
Angelou 131.

3
Angelou 179.

4
Angelou 84.

5
Angelou 11.

6
Angelou 11.

7
Angelou 2.

8
Angelou 11.

9
Angelou 11.

10
Angelou 180.

11
Angelou 63.

12
Angelou 63.

13
Angelou 64.

14
Angelou 197.

15
Angelou 2.

16
Angelou 151.

17
Angelou 151.

18
Angelou 152.

19
Angelou 152.

20
Angelou 152.

21
Angelou 155.

22
Angelou 156.

23
Angelou 101.

24
Angelou 40.

25
Angelou 157.

26
Angelou 39.

27
Angelou 26.

28
Angelou 160.

29
Angelou 161.

30
Angelou 162.

31
Angelou 16-17.

32
Angelou 77.

33
Angelou 79.

34
Angelou 156.

35
Angelou 114.

36
Angelou 45

37
Angelou 45.

38
Angelou 187.

39
Angelou 26.

40
Angelou 24.

41
Angelou 159.

42
Angelou 22.

43
Angelou 7.

44
Angelou 101.

45
Angelou 108.

46
Angelou 110.

47
Angelou 14.

48
Angelou 14.

49
Angelou 22.

50
Angelou 22.

51
Angelou 92.

52
Angelou 99-100.

53
Angelou 180.

54
Angelou 181.

55
Angelou 227.

56
Angelou 227.

57
Angelou 227.

58
Angelou 227.

59
Angelou 229.

60
Angelou 102.

61
Angelou 159.

62
Angelou 156.

Chapter 7

1
John O. Killens, "The Black Writer and the Revolution," *Arts and Society* 5 (1968): 397.

2
John O. Killens, *The Cotillion* (New York: Pocket Books, 1972) 13, 12. All subsequent citations are from *The Cotillion*.

3
Killens 12.

4
Killens 13.

5
Killens 66.

6
Killens 245.

7
Killens 245.

8
Killens 56.

9
Killens 52.

10
Killens 63.

11
Killens 63.

12
Killens 246.

13
Killens 246.

14
Killens 202, 56.

15
Killens 59.

16
Killens 186.

17
Killens 187.

18
Killens 37.

19
Killens 157.

20
Killens 35, 50.

21
Killens 15.

22
Killens 35.

23
Killens 36.

24
Killens 36, 37.

25
Killens 48.

26
Killens 15.

27
Killens 18.

28
Killens 31.

29
Killens 31.

30
Killens 31.

31
Killens 47.

32
Killens 47.

33
Killens 54.

34
Killens 157.

35
Killens 51.

36
Killens 30.

37
Killens 59.

38
Killens 87.

39
Killens 89.

40
Killens 88.

41
Killens 66.

42
Killens 66.

43
Killens 71.

44
Killens 75.

45
Killens 29.

46
Killens 75.

47
Killens 158.

48
Killens 158.

49
Killens 164.

50
Killens 172.

51
Killens 174.

52
Killens 203.

53
Killens 203.

54
Killens 250.

55
Killens 251.

56
Killens 252.

57
Killens 254-55.

58
Killens 259.

59
Killens 240.

60
Killens 240.

61
Killens 243.

62
Killens 243.

63
Killens 173.

64
Killens 247-48.

65
Killens 246.

66
Killens 287.

67
Killens 287.

69
Killens 287.

Chapter 8

1
Haki R. Madhubuti (Don L. Lee), *Think Black*, (Detroit: Broadside, 1969) 6.

2
Haki R. Madhubuti (Don L. Lee), *Don't Cry, Scream*, (Detroit: Broadside, 1970) 17.

3
Gwendolyn Brooks et al, *A Capsule Course in Black Poetry Writing* (Detroit: Broadside, 1975) 32.

4
Sonia Sanchez, *A Blues Book for Blue Black Magical Women* (Detroit: Broadside, 1974) 12.

5
Sonia Sanchez, ed, *We Be Word Sorcerers* (New York: Bantam, 1973) IX.

6
Sanchez, *We Be Word Sorcerers* X.

7
Mari Evans, *I Am a Black Woman* (New York: William Morrow, 1970) 91.

8
Madhubuti, *Think Black* 6.

9
Haki R. Madhubuti (Don L. Lee), *Black Pride* (Detroit: Broadside, 1969) 24.

10
Madhubuti, *Black Pride* 24.

11
Madhubuti, *Black Pride* 25.

12
Madhubuti, *Black Pride* 24.

13
Madhubuti, *Black Pride* 25.

14
Madhubuti, *Black Pride* 24.

15
Madhubuti, *Black Pride* 25.

16
Haki R. Madhubuti (Don L. Lee), *We Walk the Way of the New World* (Detroit: Broadside, 1970) 21.

17
Haki R. Madhubuti (Don L. Lee), *Book of Life* (Detroit: Broadside, 1973) 32.

18
Sonia Sanchez, *Homecoming* (Detroit: Broadside, 1969) 18-19.

19
Sonia Sanchez, *We a BaddDDD People* (Detroit: Broadside, 1970) 33.

20
Sanchez, *We a BaddDDD People* 33.

21
Sanchez, *We a BaddDDD People* 50.

22
Sanchez, *We a BaddDDD People* 70-71.

23
Sanchez, *A Blues Book* 61.

24
Sanchez, *We a BaddDDD People* 38-39.

25
Sanchez, *Homecoming* 29.

26
Sanchez, *We a BaddDDD People* 30.

27
Sanchez, *We a BaddDDD People* 30.

28
Madhubuti, *Don't Cry, Scream* 49.

29
Madhubuti, *We Walk the Way* 37.

30
Madhubuti, *We Walk the Way* 38.

31
Madhubuti, *We Walk the Way* 38.

32
Sanchez, We a BaddDDD People 30.

33
Sanchez, *We a BaddDDD People* 30.

34
Sanchez, *We a BaddDDD People* 31.

35
Madhubuti, *Black Pride* 25.

36
Madhubuti, *Black Pride* 25.

37
Madhubuti, *We Walk the Way* 62.

38
Madhubuti, *We Walk the Way* 63.

39
Madhubuti, *Don't Cry, Scream* 54.

40
Madhubuti, *Book of Life* 21.

41
Madhubuti, *Book of Life* 21.

42
Sanchez, *We a BaddDDD People* 14.

43
Sanchez, *We a BaddDDD People* 38.

44
Madhubuti, *Don't Cry, Scream* 39.

45
Madhubuti, *We Walk the Way* 31.

46
Madhubuti, *We Walk the Way* 32.

47
Madhubuti, *We Walk the Way* 32.

48
Madhubuti, *We Walk the Way* 32.

49
Madhubuti, *Black Pride* 30.

50
Madhubuti, *Black Pride* 30.

51
Madhubuti, *Black Pride* 31.

52
Madhubuti, *Don't Cry, Scream* 33.

53
Madhubuti, *Don't Cry, Scream* 33.

54
Sanchez, *Homecoming* 16.

55
Sanchez, *Homecoming* 16.

56
Madhubuti, *Don't Cry, Scream* 20.

57
Madhubuti, *Don't Cry, Scream* 20.

58
Haki R. Madhubuti (Don L. Lee), *Directionscore: Selected and New Poems* (Detroit: Broadside, 1971) 204.

59
Sanchez, *We a BaddDDD People* 58.

60
Sanchez, *Homecoming* 30.

61
Sanchez, *Homecoming* 30.

62
Sanchez, *Homecoming* 30.

63
Madhubuti, *Black Pride* 20.

64
Madhubuti, *Black Pride* 20.

65
Madhubuti, *Think Black* 7.

66
Sanchez, *Homecoming* 9.

67
Sanchez, *A Blues Book* 31.

68
Sanchez, *A Blues Book* 34.

69
Sanchez, *A Blues Book* 35.

70
Sanchez, *A Blues Book* 36.

71
Sanchez, *A Blues Book* 37.

72
Sanchez, *A Blues Book* 37.

Conclusion

1
Lerone Bennett, Jr., *The Shaping of Black America* (Chicago: Johnson, 1975) 229.

2
William Strickland, "The Road Since Brown: The Americanization of the Race," *Black Scholar* 11. 1 (1979): 4.

3
Vincent Harding, *There is a River: The Black Struggle for Freedom in America* (New York: Harcourt Brace Jovanovich, 1981) XII.

About the Author

Fred L. Hord earned his Ph.D. in Black Studies from Union Graduate School. Dr. Hord has written articles for the *Western Journal of Black Studies, Black Books Bulletin, Malcolm X Newsletter, Obsidian II* and *Black American Literature Forum.* He is also the author of *After H(ours)*, a poetry chapbook published by Third World Press. In addition, he is co-editor of a monograph from a 1982 symposium at Frostburg State University. Dr. Hord is a professor of literature at Knox College in Illinois.

ALSO AVAILABLE FROM THIRD WORLD PRESS

Nonfiction

*The Destruction Of Black
Civilization: Great Issues
Of A Race From 4500 B.C.
To 2000 A.D.*
by Dr. Chancellor Williams
paper $16.95
cloth $29.95

*The Isis Papers:
The Keys to the Colors*
Dr. Frances Cress Welsing
paper $14.95
cloth $29.95

*The Cultural Unity Of
Black Africa*
by Cheikh Anta Diop $14.95

Home Is A Dirty Street
by Useni Eugene Perkins $9.95

*Black Men: Obsolete, Single,
Dangerous?*
by Haki R. Madhubuti
paper $14.95
cloth $29.95

*From Plan To Planet
Life Studies: The Need
For Afrikan Minds And
Institutions*
by Haki R. Madhubuti $7.95

Enemies: The Clash Of Races
by Haki R. Madhubuti $12.95

*Kwanzaa: A Progressive And
Uplifting African-American
Holiday*
by Institute of Positive Education
Intro. by Haki R. Madhubuti $2.50

*Harvesting New Generations:
The Positive Development Of
Black Youth*
by Useni Eugene Perkins $12.95

*Confusion By Any Other Name: Essays
Exploring the Negative Impact of The
Blackman's Guide to Understanding
the Blackwoman*
Ed. Haki R. Madhubuti $3.95

*Explosion Of Chicago
Black Street Gangs*
by Useni Eugene Perkins $6.95

*The Psychopathic Racial
Personality And Other Essays*
by Dr. Bobby E. Wright $5.95

*Black Women, Feminism And Black
Liberation: Which Way?*
by Vivian V. Gordon $5.95

Black Rituals
by Sterling Plumpp $8.95

*The Redemption Of Africa
And Black Religion*
by St. Clair Drake $6.95

How I Wrote Jubilee
by Margaret Walker $1.50

Fiction, Poetry and Drama

*Mostly Womenfolk And A Man
Or Two: A Collection*
by Mignon Holland Anderson $5.95

The Brass Bed and Other Stories
Pearl Cleage $8.00

To Disembark
by Gwendolyn Brooks $6.95

Earthquakes and Sunrise Missions
By Haki R. Madhubuti $8.95

I've Been A Woman
by Sonia Sanchez $7.95

My One Good Nerve
by Ruby Dee $8.95

Geechies
by Gregory Millard $5.95

Earthquakes And Sunrise Missions
by Haki R. Madhubuti $8.95

Killing Memory: Seeking Ancestors
(Lotus Press)
by Haki R. Madhubuti $8.00

Say That The River Turns:
The Impact Of Gwendolyn Brooks
(Anthology)
Ed.by Haki R. Madhubuti $8.95

Octavia And Other Poems
by Naomi Long Madgett $8.00

A Move Further South
by Ruth Garnett $7.95

Manish
by Alfred Woods $8.00

New Plays for the Black Theatre
(Anthology)
edited by Woodie King, Jr. $14.95

So Far, So Good
Gil Scott-Heron $8.00

Wings Will Not Be Broken
Darryl Holmes $8.00

Children's Books
The Afrocentric Self Discovery and
Inventory Workbook
By Useni Perkins $5.95

The Day They Stole
The Letter J
by Jabari Mahiri $3.95

The Tiger Who Wore
White Gloves
by Gwendolyn Brooks $6.95

A Sound Investment
by Sonia Sanchez $2.95

I Look At Me
by Mari Evans $2.50

The Story of Kwanzaa
by Safisha Madhubuti $5.95

Black Books Bulletin
A limited number of back issues
of this unique journal are available
at $3.00 each:

Vol. 1, Fall '71	Interview with Hoyt W. Fuller
Vol. 1, No. 3	Interview with Lerone Bennett, Jr.
Vol. 5, No. 3	Science & Struggle
Vol. 5, No. 4	Blacks & Jews
Vol. 7, No. 3	The South

Order from Third World Press, 7524 S. Cottage Grove Ave. Chicago, IL 60619. Shipping: Add $2.50 for first book and .50 for each additional book. Mastercard/Visa orders may be placed by calling 1(312) 651-0700.